THE DUMBEST IDEA EVER!

BY
JIMMY GOWNLEY

"Cartoonists don't live anywhere. They aren't real people."
— Charles M. Schulz

This book is dedicated to the memory of Tony Graziano (1972–1994).

And to all the Girardville kids . . . past, present, and future.

Library of Congress Control Number: 2013939128

ISBN 978-0-545-45346-2 (hardcover)
ISBN 978-0-545-45347-9 (paperback)

10 9 8 7 15 16 17 18
Printed in China 38

First edition, March 2014
Edited by Adam Rau
Book design by Phil Falco
Creative Director: David Saylor
I hope you're having fun.

SKITCH
SKITCH
SKITCH
GENIUS at WORK
3:25
JIMMY?
WE **CAN'T** SEE YOUR ***FACE.***
GENIUS at WORK
3:26

SORRY! IS THIS ANY BETTER?
3:26

GREAT! AFTER ALL, WE NEED TO SEE THE BOY BEHIND THE BOOK.
OH, OKAY.

SO, JIMMY JUST TO DOUBLE CHECK...
THIS COMIC BOOK OF YOURS... YOU WROTE IT, DREW IT, AND PUBLISHED IT YOURSELF?

WELL, MY PARENTS HELPED ME GET IT PRINTED, BUT I DID THE REST MYSELF.
PRETTY IMPRESSIVE.
THANKS.

UMM... I'M REALLY NERVOUS.
I'VE NEVER BEEN INTERVIEWED ON TV BEFORE.

JUST RELAX AND BE YOURSELF.
FIRST, CAN YOU SPELL YOUR NAME FOR US?
JAY-EYE-EM-EM-WHY--GEE-OH-DOUBLE YOU-EN-EL-EEE-WHY.

AND THAT'S PRONOUNCED?
GOWN.
LEE.
LIKE "WEDDING GOWN."
...AND "STAN LEE."

"OKAY, SO JIMMY... AT JUST FIFTEEN YOU'VE WRITTEN AND PUBLISHED YOUR FIRST COMIC BOOK..."

...NOW THAT COMIC IS GOING INTO ITS SECOND PRINTING, AND YOU'RE ALREADY MAKING ANOTHER ONE.
THAT'S RIGHT.

THAT'S PRETTY CREATIVE FOR SOMEONE YOUR AGE.
SO TELL ME...
...WHERE DO YOU GET YOUR IDEAS?

OH! UMM... WELL...

"...THAT'S A GOOD QUESTION."
TWO YEARS EARLIER...
HE thanked GOD above for the DREAM his child haaaaad...

...DON'T GO DOWN IN THE MIIIIIINE, DAD
JIMMY! THERE YOU ARE!

IT'S ABOUT TIME YOU GOT HOME. SAY HELLO TO YOUR AUNTS AND UNCLES.
HELLO, AUNTS AND UNCLES.

MERRY CHRISTMAS!
YOU'RE MISSING THE SING-ALONG.
WE JUST FINISHED "DON'T GO DOWN IN THE MINE, DAD."

YEAH, I HEARD... THE WHOLE STREET HEARD.
Y'KNOW, MOST FAMILIES SING CHRISTMAS CAROLS...
NOT SONGS ABOUT 19TH CENTURY MINING DISASTERS.

SO, WHAT WERE YOU DOING OUT SO LATE? ROBBING A BANK?

HA-HA
NO!
I WAS JUST DOWN THE STREET LOOKING FOR *MARNIE MARQUARDT*.

THE GIRL FROM THE NEXT BLOCK?
I THOUGHT SHE MOVED AWAY.

SHE DID, BUT HER AUNT SAID SHE WAS GONNA VISIT HER GRANDMA TODAY.
I WENT BY THE HOUSE BUT ALL OF THE LIGHTS WERE OUT.

AWW..., I BET YOU MISS YOUR LITTLE GIRLFRIEND.

SHE WAS NOT MY GIRLFRIEND!

AND YES.

DID YOU HAVE A NICE CHRISTMAS?
OH, YEAH! I GOT A REAL ART DESK...
...AND TONS OF GRAPHIC NOVELS.
"GRAPHIC NOVELS?"
BIG, THICK COMIC BOOKS... THEY COST A FORTUNE.
WELL, HE DESERVED A GOOD CHRISTMAS. HIS REPORT CARD WAS STRAIGHT As AGAIN.
AND NOT JUST STRAIGHT As... STRAIGHT 99s!
THE PRINCIPAL SAID HE'S GIFTED.
ACTUALLY, I SHOULD HAVE GOTTEN STRAIGHT 100s, BUT SISTER REBEKAH SAID ONLY GOD IS PERFECT.
DESPITE WHAT MY GRADES SUGGEST.
SO, YOU GOT DOCKED A POINT FOR NOT BEING GOD?
YEP.
TOUGH SCHOOL.
YOU'RE TELLING ME.
WITH GRADES LIKE THAT, YOU MUST STUDY A LOT.
WHEN DO YOU HAVE TIME FOR FUN?
WELL, I STAY UP LATE...

"...REALLY LATE."
HOLY COW!
THAT STORY WAS AWESOME!

AND THE ART... IT'S MIND-BLOWING.
MEANWH
ZAP!
AARRGH!
I COULD NEVER DRAW LIKE THAT.

I HAVE TONS OF NOTEBOOKS FILLED WITH DRAWINGS...

...BUT NOTHING I DO LOOKS RIGHT.

I WISH THIS DUMB TOWN HAD A PLACE WHERE I COULD TAKE ART LESSONS.
OR AN ART STORE WHERE I COULD GET DECENT SUPPLIES.

OR AT LEAST HAD...
...I DON'T KNOW...

...AT LEAST HAD SOMETHING.

THE TRUTH IS, GIRARDVILLE IS JUST A SLATE-GRAY SCRAMBLE OF ROW HOMES AND ROCKS PLOPPED IN THE MIDDLE OF PENNSYLVANIA'S COAL REGION.
WELCOME TO
Girardville
ESTABLISHED 1832

IT'S HOME TO SIX CHURCHES...

OPEN
...SEVENTEEN BARS...

...ZERO LIBRARIES...

...AND *ME*.
HEY!
HEY!
Hawks
21

I'M OPEN!
I'M OPEN!
FRANKIE!
BUMP
SWISH!
BZZZZZZZZZZZZ

WE DID IT!
WE'RE GOING TO THE CHAMPIONSHIP!
D-FENSE!
GO TEAM
Hawks Rule
GO 4 IT!
#1

I CAN'T BELIEVE IT!
I KNOW, AFTER THREE YEARS OF PLAYING TOGETHER, WE MIGHT WIN IT ALL.

WHADDYA MEAN "MIGHT"? WE WILL WIN IT ALL!
YOU KNOW IT!

WE'RE THE BEST TEAM IN THE WORLD!

ACTUALLY, MIKE, WE'RE ONLY THE BEST OUT OF SIX SMALL SCHOOLS IN OUR CATHOLIC LEAGUE.
WELL, THAT'S BETTER THAN NOTHING!

NICE GAME, JIMMY!
MOM!
DAD!
YOU GUYS KNOW WHAT THIS MEANS, RIGHT? WE'RE IN THE LEAGUE CHAMPIONSHIP!
WE KNOW! AGAINST HOLY FAMILY. DO YOU THINK YOU CAN WIN?
ARE YOU KIDDING?
IT'S IN THE BAG!

WELCOME BACK, CLASS.

I'D LIKE TO CONGRATULATE OUR IMMACULATE HEART HAWKS ON THEIR WIN THIS SUNDAY...

...AND MR. GOWNLEY...
...I UNDERSTAND YOU SCORED *SIXTEEN POINTS!*

EIGHTEEN POINTS, SISTER REBEKAH!

EIGHTEEN POINTS!
CONGRATULATIONS.
THANK YOU, SISTER REBEKAH.

UNFORTUNATELY, I ALSO NEED TO NOTE THAT WE HAVE SIX STUDENTS OUT WITH CHICKEN POX.
I'M GOING TO HAVE TO TAKE A MOMENT TO RETHINK MY LESSON PLAN.
SO, EVERYONE CAN USE THIS PERIOD TO *READ* INDEPENDENTLY.

AHEM!
MR. GOWNLEY! DO YOU SERIOUSLY BELIEVE...
THAT A CARTOON BOOK...
...IS APPROPRIATE FOR A CLASSROOM?
SNATCH
SEE ME AFTER SCHOOL!
BUT SISTER, I THINK--
AFTER SCHOOL!
HEE HEE
SNICKER
giggle
TEE HEE

HAHAHAHAHA
HAHAHAHAHAHAHA

RRRRIIIIIINNG!

YOU...
...YOU WANTED TO SEE ME, SISTER?
YES.

MR. GOWNLEY, AS THE TOP STUDENT IN THIS CLASS, I EXPECT MORE FROM YOU.

TRASH LIKE THIS IS NEVER ACCEPTABLE IN THIS CLASSROOM.
TOMORROW, BRING IN SOMETHING MORE APPROPRIATE FOR SCHOOL.
YES, SISTER.

ACTUALLY, SISTER... I THINK THIS IS APPROPRIATE.
...I THINK IT'S GREAT.

OH, PLEASE! YOU ARE SUCH A GOOD READER! WHY WASTE YOUR TIME WITH JUNK?

I KNOW I'M A GOOD READER! HOW DO YOU THINK I GOT THAT WAY?

YOU "GOT THAT WAY" BECAUSE OF YOUR TEACHERS! SISTER RUTH! MRS. EICHE! MISS KLINGER!
BATMAN!

"BATMAN"?
YEAH! YOU KNOW...

...THE PEOPLE WHO WORK ON BATMAN! THE WRITERS! GAH! YOU KNOW, WHAT I MEAN!

WELL, DON'T GET ANGRY.

I'M NOT ANGRY!
I'M JUST...
FRUSTRATED!

OKAY. SETTLE DOWN.
I HAVE AN IDEA.

LATER...
SCHUYLKILL MALL
COME VISIT OUR FAMILY OF STORES
...AND SHE SAID THAT THE WHOLE CLASS IS GOING TO BE GIVING ORAL REPORTS NEXT WEEK ANYWAY.

AND MINE SHOULD BE ABOUT THE VALUE OF COMIC BOOKS IN EDUCATION.
WAIT! THE WHOLE CLASS HAS TO DO THESE THINGS?

YEAH, SHE'S GONNA ANNOUNCE IT TOMORROW ANYWAY, SO SHE JUST TOLD ME EARLY.

THAT STINKS! THE CHAMPIONSHIP IS NEXT FRIDAY.
WE NEED TO FOCUS.

I KNOW, FRANKIE, BUT MY PRESENTATION HAS TO BE GREAT.
I WANT HER TO SEE HOW WRONG SHE WAS TO YELL AT ME LIKE THAT.

SHUT UP!
LOOK WHO'S COMING...

... ANDY COSTA, TONY GRAZIANO, AND MIKE MOHUTSKY.

THEY PLAY FOR HOLY FAMILY AND ARE THEREFORE COMPLETELY EVIL.

HEY, GUYS!
gate
GOOD LUCK IN THE GAME NEXT WEEK. MAY THE BEST TEAM WIN.

SEE WHAT I MEAN?

JIMMY, WE ORDERED PIZZA, DO YOU WANT SOME?
YEAH! THANKS!

YOU'RE STILL WORKING ON THAT PRESENTATION? YOU'VE BEEN AT IT FOR DAYS.
YOU'LL DEFINITELY GET AN A WITH ALL OF THE WORK YOU PUT IN.

THIS ISN'T ABOUT THE GRADE.
I'M TRYING TO PROVE A POINT.

SIGH
YOU'RE YOUR FATHER ALL OVER AGAIN.

WELL, WE SEEM TO HAVE TEMPORARILY LOST A FEW MORE TO CHICKEN POX...

...BUT I'M HAPPY TO SEE CHRIS McCONNELL BACK AFTER JUST THREE DAYS.

SO, DESPITE THE MANY ABSENCES, WHAT SAY WE PRESS ON WITH OUR PRESENTATIONS?

WHO WANTS TO GO *FIRST*?
OOH! ME! ME!

MISTER GOWNLEY...
...THE FLOOR IS YOURS.

-AHEM-
GRAPHIC LITERATURE... MORE COMMONLY KNOWN BY THE MISLEADING TERM "COMIC BOOK"... IS ONE OF AMERICA'S FEW IN... IN... INDIGENOUS ART FORMS.
Presentation TODAY!
IT... UMM... IT IS A MULTIMILLION-DOLLAR INDUSTRY THAT EMPLOYS SOME OF OUR COUNTRY'S GREATEST WRITERS AND ARTISTS.
COMICS HAVE BEEN USED BY OUR ARMED FORCES TO TRAIN SOLDIERS...
...AND BY TEACHERS TO HELP IMMIGRANT CHILDREN LEARN ENGLISH.

TODAY I'M GOING TO TALK SPECIFICALLY ABOUT COMICS' POTENTIAL ROLE IN EDUCATION.
BUT FIRST...

...A DRAMATIC READING.

AND BOY, WAS IT...
THERE WERE...
CHARTS!
Category 4
Category 3
Category 2
Category 1
Column1
Intelligence
Comics read
2 4 6 8 10 12
COMICS ARE GOOD, AND GOOD FOR YOU!
IT SAYS SO ON THIS CHART! YA GONNA ARGUE WITH A CHART?
ZIP!
HEARTFELT! PERSONAL! PLEAS!
SOB!
PLEASE -SOB- COMICS CAN SAVE A LIFE!
MAYBE YOUR LIFE -SOB- -SOB-

SINGING AND DANCING
HELLO, MY COMICS
HELLO, MY FUNNIES
HELLO, MY NEWSPRINT PALS
ZOOM!!
ERT!
THANK YOU, GIRARDVILLE!
GOOD NIGHT!
IF I COULD SUM IT UP IN TWO WORDS?
AWE. SOME.

SO, AT THE END OF THE DAY...
MISTER GOWNLEY?
YES, SISTER?
I JUST WANTED TO TELL YOU THAT YOUR TALK WAS WONDERFUL!
SCRATCH
YOU HAD EXCELLENT ARGUMENTS, STRONG RESEARCH, AND YOU PRESENTED IT WELL.
YOU CAN EXPECT A VERY HIGH A.
WOW!
THANK YOU! THAT'S GREAT!
SCRATCH SCRATCH
SO, WE CAN READ COMICS IN THE CLASSROOM NOW?
WHAT?
NO.
OF COURSE NOT.
YOUR PRESENTATION WAS GOOD...
BUT I'M NOT ABOUT TO CHANGE MY POLICIES.
SCRATCH

BUT, YOU SAID IT WAS EXCELLENT!
YES, BUT--
YOU SAID IT WAS WONDERFUL!
WELL, IT WAS.

THEN WHAT IS WRONG--
MISTER GOWNLEY!

YOUR PRESENTATION WAS WELL DONE. YOU WILL RECEIVE AN A FOR YOUR WORK.
BUT THAT.
IS.
ALL.

YES, SISTER.
I UNDERSTAND.
SCRATCH SCRATCH

HOW DID THE PRESENTA--
I DON'T WANNA TALK ABOUT IT!

WHAT A CROCK!

WHAT WAS THE POINT OF ALL THAT WORK? WHY DID I TRY SO HARD? WHY DID I CARE SO MUCH?
SCRATCH
SCRATCH

AND WHY AM I SO FREAKING ITCHY?!
SCRATCH
SCRATCH
SCRATCH
SCRATCH
SCRATCH
SCRATCH

oh no.

I CAN PLAY!

YOU CAN'T PLAY. YOU'RE CONTAGIOUS.
RIGHT.

LOOK, I'LL GO TO THE GAME AND CALL EVERY FEW MINUTES TO GIVE YOU AN UPDATE, OKAY?

AND BETWEEN YOUR DAD'S CALLS, WE CAN SAY A ROSARY THAT NO ONE GETS HURT!

DAD?

CALL OFTEN.

THIS IS AWFUL!
I'M THE TEAM'S LEADING SCORER.
I SHOULD BE PLAYING!

YOU'RE SICK! YOU'D INFECT EVERYBODY!
GOOD! I COULD INFECT THE OTHER TEAM AND WATCH THEM SCRATCH THEMSELVES DOWN TO TINY LOSER NUBS.

JUST RELAX AND DRAW. I'M SURE YOUR DAD WILL CALL AGAIN--
RRIIING
RRIIING

HELLO?
HELLO, DAD?

UH-HUH!
UH-HUH!
AWESOME!

WE'RE UP EIGHT WITH TWO MINUTES TO GO IN THE FOURTH...

WE CAN'T LOSE.
HAWKS
HEY, MOM... IF I GET THIS *FINISHED*, WILL YOU TAKE IT DOWN TO SCHOOL TOMORROW FOR THE GUYS?
SURE, JIMMY...
...BUT MAYBE YOU SHOULD WAIT TO FINISH IT...
Y'KNOW... WHEN YOU KNOW YOU'VE WON.
MOMMM!
YOU'RE *SUCH* A WORRY-WORT!
I JUST DON'T WANT YOU TO BE UPSET IF SOMETHING *BAD* HAPPENS.
BUT IT *IS* NICE TO SEE YOU *HAPPY*.

I GUESS I AM. THERE'S JUST ONE THING...

...I DIDN'T GET TO BE A PART OF IT.

JIMMY! THAT'S NOT TRUE! YOU WERE A BIG PART OF THE WHOLE SEASON!

YEAH, BUT NOT THE CHAMPIONSHIP!
CHAMPIONS

SO, WHO CARES ABOUT--
RRRIIIING
ZIP
TINK

DAD? WHAT'S--
WHAT?!

IT'S TIED!
WITH A MINUTE LEFT!

NO! DON'T HANG UP! I'LL STAY ON AND LISTEN!

WHAT'S THAT?! WHO'S CHEERING?!
DID WE--?

OH...

"..WE LOST."
CHAMPIONS

ABSENT FOR TWO WHOLE *WEEKS*.
AND I'M STILL COVERED IN ALL THESE *SPOTS*.
UGH!
BUT EVEN IF I'M A MESS, IT'LL BE GOOD TO GET BACK TO SCHOOL.

EVEN IF I STILL DON'T FEEL GREAT.

SIGH

MAYBE I JUST NEED TO GET BACK INTO A ROUTINE.

HEY, FRANKIE. HEY, MIKE.
LOOK! HE'S BACK FROM THE DEAD!
HEY, SICK BOY... I MADE YOU A CARD.
"ROSES ARE RED. VIOLETS ARE BLUE...
...WE LOST THE CHAMPIONSHIP BECAUSE OF YOU."
HA. FUNNY.
HEY, SICK
DON'T BE UPSET. I WAS ONLY KIDDING!
ARE YOU OKAY?
YEAH... NO... I KNOW! I'M JUST NOT MYSELF... YET, I GUESS. BUT... UHH... I...UHH...
BLAUGH
OKAY... I'M FINE NOW...
...JUST NEEDED...
...NEEDED...
WELL, THAT'S NOT GOOD.
THUD

IT'S PNEUMONIA.

HE WON'T NEED TO BE HOSPITALIZED AT THIS STAGE...

...BUT HE WILL BE OUT OF SCHOOL FOR A WHILE...

AT LEAST A WEEK OR TWO FOR SOMETHING LIKE THIS.

SIGH

MOAN!
A MONTH.
BETWEEN THIS AND CHICKEN POX, IT'LL BE A MONTH OF LYING ON THIS DUMB *COUCH*.

NO FUN. NO FRIENDS. NO SPORTS... *NOTHING*!
AND WHEN I GET BETTER... *THEN* WHAT?
EVERYTHING JUST GOES BACK TO THE WAY IT *WAS*?

THE *SCHOOL*, THE *PRESSURE*, THE *EXPECTATIONS*... IT'S ALL GONNA COME BACK.
NO.

NO. I'M JUST GONNA FORGET IT ALL.
I'M JUST GONNA LIE HERE UNTIL I DIE.

MOAN!
BLOINK!
We need to TALK.

is this... it?
is this... my time?

Dude, GET a GRIP! You're NOT DYING!
You have, like, a BAD COLD or something.
Chill out.

IF I'M NOT DYING, WHY ARE YOU HERE?

HONestly?
It's the CONSTANT whining!
I heard THAT, and figured someone really WAS dying...
...but, I GET here...

... and it's just YOU.
GEE. SORRY TO DISAPPOINT YOU!

LOOK, you want some FREE ADVICE?
You need to LIGHTEN UP.
You put too much PRESSURE on yourself.

Not everything has to be so... GRIM... y'know?

You're NOT DYING. In fact, your whole LIFE is ahead of you...
...any life you WANT, actually.
All you have to do...

...is LIVE it.

HONESTLY? I'M GETTING WORRIED. I THINK HE'S TALKING TO HIMSELF.
OKAY. I'LL TELL HIM.

JIMMY, IT'S YOUR COUSIN ANN MARIE. SHE WANTS TO KNOW HOW YOU'RE FEELING.

=SIGH= WELL, SHE SAID TO TURN ON CHANNEL 4. THERE'S A SHOW ON YOU MIGHT LIKE.

=CLICK=

Comic books, those brightly colored pamphlets traditionally read by children, half-wits, and the criminally insane, have been getting a makeover lately.

Joining us today to talk about this, let's go with "interesting," art form, is Gene Suzko, owner of GeMa Books... a comic book store located in Wilkes Barre, PA.

Gene, tell me, aren't comic books just dumbed-down fantasies for arrested adolescents afraid to leave their mothers' basements?

Not at all, Steve. In my shop we sell comics and graphic novels on all sorts of topics that appeal to a wide variety of readers.
Mushy
Stuff
Wow

WHAT ARE YOU WATCHING?
DAD! IT'S A WHOLE SHOW ABOUT COMICS!
AND THERE'S A GUY ON WHO HAS A STORE THAT JUST SELLS COMIC BOOKS!

IT'S AMAZING! LOOK AT ALL THOSE BOOKS! I HAVEN'T HEARD OF HALF OF THEM.

WELL, IT LOOKS LIKE IT'S UP IN WILKES-BARRE. THAT'S JUST OVER AN HOUR AWAY...
...WE CAN GO SOMETIME, IF YOU WANT.

THAT'S AWESOME!
CAN WE GO THIS WEEKEND?

WELL...
I GUESS...
BUT...UH...

AREN'T YOU SUPPOSED TO BE DYING?

OH!
UHH...

IT'S A MIRACLE!

GOOD MORNING, SISTER. HERE ARE ALL MY ASSIGNMENTS.
MISTER GOWNLEY, NICE TO HAVE YOU BACK.
YOU CAN TAKE YOUR SEAT.

YOU'RE ALIVE... UHH... AGAIN.
MOSTLY.

THANKS FOR BRINGING ALL MY ASSIGNMENTS HOME FOR ME, FRANKIE.

SURE! I KNOW HOW IMPORTANT YOUR GRADES ARE TO YOU.
ARE THEY?

UMM... WELL... SPEAKING OF ASSIGNMENTS... WHAT HISTORIC EVENT DID YOU PICK FOR YOUR ESSAY?

WAIT!
WHAT WHAT DID I PICK FOR MY WHAT?!

THE ESSAY! IT WAS IN THE PACK OF ASSIGNMENTS I BROUGHT TO YOUR HOUSE.
IT'S DUE TODAY NO EXCEPTIONS.

OH, SHOOT!
I NEED TO THINK FAST.

OR NOT.
BETTER JUST SCRIBBLE SOMETHING DOWN...
... AND HOPE FOR THE BEST.

TWO DAYS LATER...

OH MY GOD.

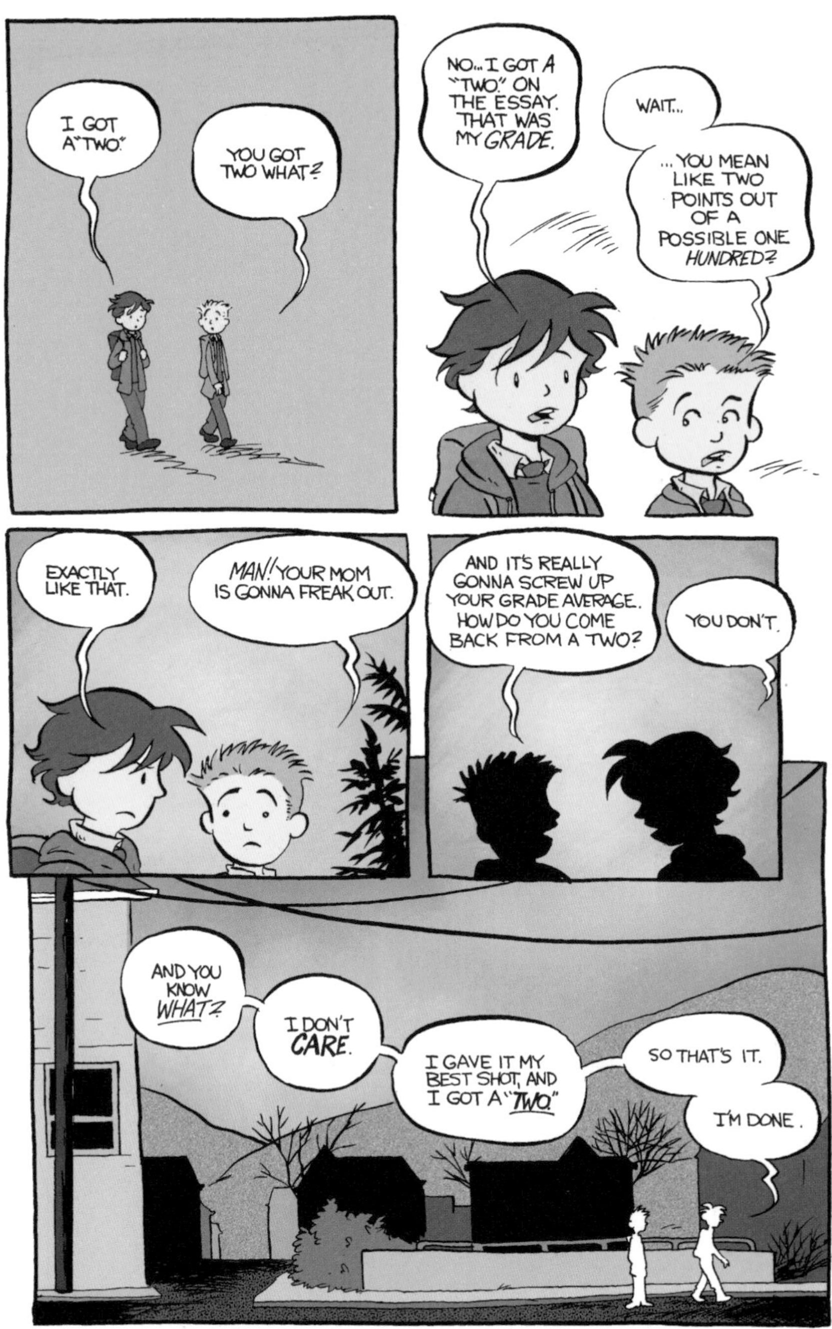
I GOT A "TWO."
YOU GOT TWO WHAT?
NO... I GOT *A* "TWO." ON THE ESSAY. THAT WAS MY *GRADE*.
WAIT...
...YOU MEAN LIKE TWO POINTS OUT OF A POSSIBLE ONE *HUNDRED*?
EXACTLY LIKE THAT.
MAN! YOUR MOM IS GONNA FREAK OUT.
AND IT'S REALLY GONNA SCREW UP YOUR GRADE AVERAGE. HOW DO YOU COME BACK FROM A TWO?
YOU DON'T.
AND YOU KNOW *WHAT?*
I DON'T **CARE**.
I GAVE IT MY BEST SHOT, AND I GOT A "*TWO.*"
SO THAT'S IT.
I'M DONE.

2/100
F
THIS IS GARBAGE!!!
COULDN'T AGREE MORE.
HI, MOM. I'M HOME.
JIMMY, HELLO! HOW WAS SCHOOL?
OH, IT WAS OKAY.
I'M GONNA GO START ON MY HOMEWORK, OKAY?
ALL RIGHT, I'LL CALL YOU FOR DINNER. WORK *HARD*.
DON'T WORRY...

...I WILL.

HMM...
IT DOESN'T LOOK LIKE MUCH...
GEMA BOOKS
...HOPE YOU'RE NOT DISAPPOINTED.

GEMA BOOKS
CLICK
CLACK

HOLEEEEE...
WARP SPEED PRESS
ROCKETS
ZOOM!
NEW THIS WEEK!
STAFF PICK
POWER
POP
MUSHY STUFF
IT'S DREAMY
GHOSTY
STICK MEN
BITE MY NOSE
SALE
ALternative COMICS
50% OFF (THIS BOX ONLY)

POW! COMIX!
ON SALE HERE
STRANGE A-
A-KAT
PESTRY
MOO HOO HA HA
WOLFMAN MODEL
T-SHIRTS
PLUSHIE

LOOK AT THIS! THERE MUST BE DOZENS OF NEW BOOKS HERE! HUNDREDS!
DOGS VS CATS
GOOD VIBES
BITE MY NOSE #1
UGH!
MEH. THE COMIC YOU CAN TAKE OR LEAVE
WHOOPIE PIE
WOW
FUNNIES
SOUP
AMAZING FOOT MAN!
KICKIN IT!
THE COMIC THAT WANTS YOU TO DROP DEAD!
SHUT UP!
STICK MEN
WINNER: BEST ARTIST!
MUSHY STUFF
AXES FOR EXES!
WONDER
MURDER MONTHLY
GHOSTY
ALL NEW
MAGIC QUEST
BORING MAN!
IT'S TAX TIME.
IT'S DREAMY
POWER!
STUPID DUMB CAT!
WAR COMICS AND HUMOR COMICS... HORROR, CRIME, SCI-FI, ROMANCE...
AND NOT ONE OF THEM LOOKS APPROPRIATE FOR A KID MY AGE.
AWESOME.

WOW. THAT'S QUITE A HAUL YOU HAVE THERE.
YEP!

I'VE NEVER BEEN TO A COMIC BOOK STORE BEFORE.
I BOUGHT ONE OF EVERYTHING I NEVER HEARD OF.

AND SOME LOOK SUPER WEIRD.
LIKE, WHAT'S THE DEAL WITH THIS ONE ABOUT THE DONKEY?

ACTUALLY, THAT'S AN AARDVARK, AND IT'S ONE OF THE BEST COMICS GOING RIGHT NOW.
BUT YOU CAN ONLY GET IT IN COMIC SHOPS.

IT'S CREATED BY THESE TWO GUYS IN CANADA, AND THERE'S NO BIG COMPANY OR ANYTHING. THEY JUST PUT IT OUT THEMSELVES.
AND THEY MAKE MONEY THAT WAY?
FLIP
NO!

ARE YOU KIDDING? FROM WHAT I'VE SEEN, THEY LIVE LIKE ROCK STARS.
HUH.

IT'S ALL SO
INCREDIBLE!

I COULD NEVER
COME UP WITH
STUFF LIKE
THIS.

MAN!

WHERE DO THEY
GET THEIR
IDEAS?

THAT SUMMER, I SPENT MORE TIME WITH THE KIDS IN MY NEIGHBORHOOD WHO WENT TO PUBLIC SCHOOL.
WE HUNG OUT. PLAYED BASKETBALL...
...AND NO ONE EVER MENTIONED SCHOOL, OR GRADES.

TWO BROTHERS, MARK AND TRACY OLSON, LIVED DOWN THE STREET FROM ME
IT WAS THERE THAT I SPENT THE MOST TIME, AND HAD THE MOST FUN.
THERE! NOW, HOP ON THE THING!
THE OTHER THING!
THE BLUE THING!
HOP! HOP! HOP!
OH, MAN! YOU SUCK AT THIS.
BEEP BOOP BLONK
I KNOW, ISN'T IT AWESOME?
BUT BEFORE I KNEW IT, SUMMER WAS OVER.
SO, WHY DOES GIRARDVILLE HAVE FIREWORKS IN AUGUST?
WERE WE LATE FOR THE REVOLUTION?
NO. THE TOWN IS JUST CHEAP.
THEY GET 'EM HALF PRICE AFTER JULY.

LAME.
YEAH. WELL, THAT'S GIRARDVILLE.
WHAT CAN YOU DO?
LEAVE.
AS SOON AS POSSIBLE.
AND GO WHERE?
NEW YORK.
HAVE YOU EVER BEEN TO NEW YORK?
NO, BUT IT'S GOTTA BE BETTER THAN HERE.
C'MON, YOU GOTTA ADMIT THIS WAS AN AWESOME SUMMER.
YEAH... MAYBE I'M JUST IN A BAD MOOD BECAUSE IT'S ALMOST OVER.
SCHOOL STARTS NEXT WEEK.

THAT'S RIGHT! YOU'RE GONNA BE A BIG HIGH SCHOOL MAN.
TOO BAD YOU'RE STILL IN CATHOLIC SCHOOL. IT'D BE COOL IF YOU WENT WITH US.

YEAH...WELL, SCHOOL IS SCHOOL, Y'KNOW?

HONESTLY, I JUST HOPE THERE ARE SOME CUTE GIRLS.

CARDINAL BRENNAN HIGH SCHOOL...

...THE FIRST PRACTICE OF THE NEW SEASON.
IT'S KIND OF WEIRD PLAYING ON THE SAME TEAM AS THE GUYS FROM HOLY FAMILY.
I MEAN THERE THEY ALL ARE... ANDY COSTA, MIKE MOHUTSKY, ALL THE GUYS WHO BEAT US.
YEAH.
AND THEY'RE ALL PRETTY NICE... THE RATS!
"AND WHAT ABOUT HIM? TONY GRAZIANO."
CHARGERS
YEAH... BUT HE IS NICE, TOO.
ARE YOU KIDDING? HE'S SMART, TEACHERS LOVE HIM, HE'S ON STUDENT COUNCIL, AND, LIKE, FIVE GIRLS HAVE CRUSHES ON HIM.
I KNOW.
THAT'S THE WORST PART.

LUNCHTIME...THE NEXT DAY...

HOW DO YOU LIKE BRENNAN SO FAR?
IT IS WHAT IT IS, Y'KNOW?
YEAH.

WHAT DO YOU GUYS THINK ABOUT MR. SHANER FOR GOVERNMENT CLASS?
HE'S TOUGH.

YEAH, BUT HE'S FAIR. I DON'T CARE IF YOU'RE TOUGH, AS LONG AS YOU'RE FAIR.
HOW ABOUT SISTER ANN JAMES?

I LIKE HER A LOT. SHE'S KIND OF A HIPPIE.

YEAH, BUT SOME OF THOSE BOOKS! I MEAN GREAT EXPECTATIONS? UGH!
THAT PIP CHARACTER NEEDS TO BE BEATEN ABOUT THE HEAD AND SHOULDERS.

YEAH, BUT IN CLASS YOU CAN ACTUALLY SAY YOU DON'T LIKE THE BOOK. SHE LETS YOU HAVE AN OPINION, AND THAT'S REALLY COOL.
TRUE.

OKAY. NO ONE'S MENTIONED THE OBVIOUS...
...ALGEBRA ONE WITH...
...SISTER REGINA ALMA.
BRRRRR...
THE VERY NAME SENDS CHILLS DOWN MY SPINE!

I HEARD SHE MADE A GIRL PEE HERSELF.
NO WAY!

DUDE, I SWEAR.
THE GIRL WAS LATE, AND REGINA ALMA FREAKED OUT ON HER.
SO THE KID SPRUNG A LEAK RIGHT THERE IN CLASS.
THAT'S AWFUL!

LIKE HER CLASS ISN'T HARD ENOUGH WITHOUT HER COMPROMISING YOUR BLADDER CONTROL.

YEAH, THE CLASS IS A NIGHTMARE.
LAST NIGHT'S HOMEWORK WAS KILLER.
WE HAD HOMEWORK?

UHH... YEAH...
LIKE TEN PROBLEMS.
SHOOT! I WASN'T PAYING ATTENTION.

DUDE, SHE IS GONNA LOSE IT.
HOPE YOU HAVE A PAIR OF DIAPERS.

SHUT UP!
IT'S NOT TILL NEXT PERIOD. I MIGHT HAVE TIME TO--

RRRIIIIING

LOOK...
...MAYBE SHE WON'T CALL ON YOU.
Yeah... maybe.

OKAY, CLASS, LET'S BEGIN BY REVIEWING LAST NIGHT'S HOMEWORK.
QUESTION ONE...
...MR. GOWNLEY.
UNBELIEVABLE.
DON'T MUMBLE, MISTER GOWNLEY!
IF YOU HAVE SOMETHING TO SAY...
...SAY IT.
YES, SISTER. IT'S JUST THAT--
PARDON ME, SISTER, I'M CONFUSED!
HOW CAN YOU BE CONFUSED, MR. GRAZIANO?
WE HAVEN'T STARTED YET.
WELL, IT'S JUST...THE WHOLE "X" THING, Y'KNOW? IN EVERY PROBLEM, WE NEED TO FIND "X," BUT WHAT IS "X"...
Y'KNOW... PHILOSOPHICALLY?

WHAT ARE YOU DOING?
JUST SHUT UP.

THAT IS THE POINT OF THE EQUATION, MR. GRAZIANO...
TO FIND WHAT "X" IS.

BUT WHY IS IT ALWAYS "X"?
WHY CAN'T IT BE SOMETHING ELSE?

THE CHOICE OF THE LETTER "X" IS IRRELEVANT! IT COULD BE "ISHKABIBBLE." IT COULD BE "BOONDOGGLE SQUARED."
DO YOU UNDERSTAND?

NOPE.
OH MY GOD, YOU'RE DEAD!

WELL, MAYBE PERSONALLY SOLVING ALL of the HOMEWORK PROBLEMS AT THE BLACKBOARD WILL HELP YOU UNDERSTAND!

AMDG
RRRRIIIING
TONY! I'M SO SORRY. YOU DIDN'T HAVE TO COVER FOR ME LIKE THAT.
YEAH, WELL YOU OWE ME ONE.
WELL, HOW ABOUT THIS?
I OFFICIALLY FORGIVE YOU FOR BEATING US IN THE EIGHTH-GRADE CHAMPIONSHIP.
oh, well... then it was WORTH it...
SEE?!

JIMMY!
THESE GRADES! YOUR CLASS RANK DROPPED BY ANOTHER THREE...
...BY ANOTHER SIX!
...ANOTHER FOUR!
I JUST DON'T UNDERSTAND. YOU'RE SUCH A SMART KID...
...WHAT'S WRONG?

WHAT'S *WRONG*? I'M *DROWNING*! I'M UNHAPPY ALL THE TIME. IT'S NOT YOUR FAULT, AND THERE'S NOTHING YOU CAN DO...
MAYBE THERE'S NOTHING ANYONE CAN DO.

BUT I'M SCARED. I FEEL LIKE I'M LOST, AND I'LL NEVER FIND MY WAY HOME AGAIN.

I'M FINE!

YOU WORRY TOO MUCH. SO, I'M HAVING SOME ISSUES AT SCHOOL.
IT'LL WORK OUT IN THE END.

NOW LOOK... TONIGHT WE HAVE TO DECORATE THE GYM FOR BRENNAN DAY.
IT'S A WHOLE SCHOOL PRIDE THING.
AND IT'S ACTUALLY KINDA *FUN*.

"...SO I'M GONNA SEE IF I CAN FIND SOME GOOD OL' SCHOOL SPIRIT."
GO CHARGERS! CB #1
BRENNAN DAY!!
Cardinal Brennan High Forever
Brennan HIGH

CHARGERS DRIVE ME "BATTY!"
CB
GOOD EVENING, MISTER GOWNLEY. HARD AT WORK?
SISTER REGINA ALMA! HI!
YEAH. I GUESS I AM.
I WANTED TO GET THREE POSTERS DONE TONIGHT.
AND I ALREADY FINISHED TWO.
SO, TWO OUT OF THREE...
... THAT'S 66.6% ISN'T IT?
YES, SISTER.
WELL, GOOD JOB...
66% IS BETTER THAN YOU DID ON TODAY'S TEST.

HAVE A NICE NIGHT.

NICE POSTERS.

DID YOU REALLY DRAW THESE?
HUH?
OH, YEAH! I DID!
THEY ARE SOOOOO COOL!
THANKS!
SUPER
I'M JIMMY GOWNLEY.
HI! I'M ELLEN TOOLE.
AND THAT'S SUPERMAN AND BATMAN, RIGHT?
YEP... WELL, THE NON-TRADEMARKED FAN VERSIONS, ANYWAY.
CB
CHARGERS DRIVE ME "BATTY!"
SO, YOU'RE INTO SUPERHEROES?
UMM... I LIKE COMIC BOOKS A LOT, AND I GUESS SOME SUPERHEROES ARE COOL.
AND SUPERMAN AND BATMAN ARE DEFINITELY THE BEST.
YEAH? WHY IS THAT?

BECAUSE THEY'RE THE FIRST, AND HAVE THE BEST SECRET ORIGINS, Y'KNOW?
I TOTALLY DON'T KNOW.

SURE YOU DO! BATMAN'S PARENTS ARE KILLED, SO HE TRAINS HIMSELF TO FIGHT CRIME. SUPERMAN'S WHOLE PLANET GETS BLOWN UP, AND HE'S SENT TO EARTH TO USE HIS POWERS TO HELP PEOPLE.
CHAR

GEEZ! THAT'S PRETTY DARK. DOESN'T ANYONE BECOME A SUPERHERO BY GOING TO A GOOD COLLEGE?
NOT THAT I'M AWARE OF, NO.
CB #1
GO CHARGERS! WIN

IT USUALLY HAS TO BE SOMETHING TRAUMATIC. SOMETHING THAT'S BAD AT FIRST, BUT THAT MAKES THE HERO BECOME WHAT HE'S SUPPOSED TO BECOME.

YEAH? SO, DO YOU HAVE A SECRET ORIGIN, CARTOON BOY?

YOU DO THAT.
HA! NOT YET, BUT I'LL KEEP YOU UPDATED.
OKAY. WELL, I GOTTA GET BACK TO MY GROUP.
RIGHT.
WELL, HAVE FUN FAKING HOW MUCH YOU LOVE SCHOOL.
FAKING?
I'M NOT FAKING. I DO LOVE SCHOOL.
?!
REALLY?
HUH.
HOW...
...WEIRD.
WHY? IT'S EASY FOR ME.
I'M GOOD AT IT.

"WHY WOULDN'T I LIKE IT?"

I'M NOT SAYING I DON'T LIKE IT. I'M JUST SAYING THAT IT'S FAKE.

INTERESTING...

HOW DO YOU MEAN?

WHAT ABOUT THE STORY IS "FAKE"?

WELL, LIKE THE WAY THE ENDING IS FORESHADOWED AT THE BEGINNING...

LIKE IT'S JUST A BIG CIRCLE.

THAT'S FAKE.

REAL LIFE DOESN'T HAVE FORESHADOWING, Y'KNOW? STUFF JUST HAPPENS.

THAT'S AN INTRIGUING STATEMENT, BUT IS IT TRUE?
KAREN?
GREAT EXPECTATIONS

I DON'T THINK SO... LIKE, IF A PERSON IS TROUBLE IN THE PAST, THEY PROBABLY WILL BE IN THE FUTURE.

INTERESTING.
YES, TONY?
THAT'S NOT EXACTLY WHAT I MEAN.
IT'S LIKE... Y'KNOW WHEN YOU'RE WATCHING A HORROR MOVIE, AND SOME GUY GOES "I FEEL LIKE I COULD LIVE FOREVER."

WELL, YOU KNOW THAT GUY'S NOT GONNA MAKE IT THROUGH THE WHOLE MOVIE! AND THAT STUFF RUINS THE WHOLE STORY FOR ME.

JIMMY, YOU HAVE A COMMENT?

I JUST THINK THAT SOMETIMES THE WRITER HAS TO USE THOSE TRICKS, OR WHATEVER, SO THAT PEOPLE CAN UNDERSTAND WHAT HE'S TRYING TO SAY...

.. AND EVEN IF IT'S NOT JUST LIKE REAL LIFE--
YOU'RE ALL MISSING the POINT!

MISTER McCONNELL, INTERRUPTING ISN'T--
IT DOESN'T MATTER ABOUT FORESHADOWING. THE POINT IS THAT THE MAIN CHARACTER IS AN IDIOT.

HE SPENDS THE FIRST PART OF THE STORY BEING ALL ARROGANT 'CUZ THINGS ARE GOING HIS WAY, BUT WHEN THINGS GET TOUGH, HE *FALLS* APART.

OKAY.
DOES A CHARACTER LIKE THAT RING TRUE TO US AS READERS?

IT DOES TO ME. I KNOW PEOPLE LIKE THAT. THERE ARE PEOPLE LIKE THAT IN THIS ROOM.

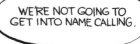

WE'RE NOT GOING TO GET INTO NAME CALLING.

I'M NOT CALLING ANYONE ***NAMES***.

BUT I KNOW PEOPLE WHO WERE HOT STUFF BEFORE HIGH SCHOOL WHO JUST CAN'T HACK IT NOW.

EVEN THE KID WHO USED TO HAVE THE HIGHEST GRADES IS NOW JUST A NOTHING.
OH, YEAH?
AND WHO ARE YOU TALKING ABOUT, CHRIS?
YOU KNOW EXACTLY WHO I'M TALKING ABOUT.
OKAY. THAT'S ENOUGH.
SISTER, I HAVE ANOTHER OBSERVATION.
CHRIS McCONNELL IS A--
RRRIIING

GEEZ! WHAT WAS *THAT* ALL ABOUT?

FRANKIE, I SWEAR I HAVE *NO IDEA*.

WERE YOU GUYS ARGUING BEFORE, OR SOMETHING?

NO. I NEVER EVEN *TALK* TO THE JERK.

SO YOU DON'T KNOW WHY HE WENT *OFF* ON YOU?

NO.

SO THE WHOLE THING CAME OUT OF NOWHERE?

YES!

SEE? I WAS RIGHT.

REAL LIFE *DOESN'T* HAVE *FORESHADOWING*.

SO, IS THIS IT?
IS THIS ALL I AM NOW?
THE KID WHO USED TO BE SPECIAL?
Great Expectations
Dickens
WHIZZZ
WAP
FLUMP
PLEASE, GOD... I AM MISERABLE...
PLEASE HELP ME FIGURE THIS OUT.
I NEED IT TO BE BETTER...
... PLEASE...

SIGH
PLOP!

NNNNNNNNN

YAWN!
CLICK

GUM

"THEY JUST PUT IT OUT THEMSELVES."
AARD

"FROM WHAT I'VE SEEN, THEY LIVE LIKE ROCK STARS."
FLIP FLIP

"SO, DO YOU HAVE A SECRET ORIGIN?"

HUH.

I COULD DO IT, COULDN'T I?
I COULD PUBLISH MY OWN COMIC BOOK.
I COULD PRINT IT, AND SELL IT... IT COULD BE A WHOLE BIG THING.
AND I HAVE EVERYTHING I NEED, TOO.
I HAVE THIS COOL DESK.
I HAVE SOME PENCILS...
...SOME PAPER.
ALL I NEED IS AN IDEA.
WHERE DO I GET AN IDEA?

9:35 PM
11:36 PM

UGH! TWO HOURS, AND THIS BLANK WHITE PAGE IS STILL BLANK AND WHITE.
I JUST NEED TO START. JUST PUT *SOMETHING* DOWN ON *PAPER*.

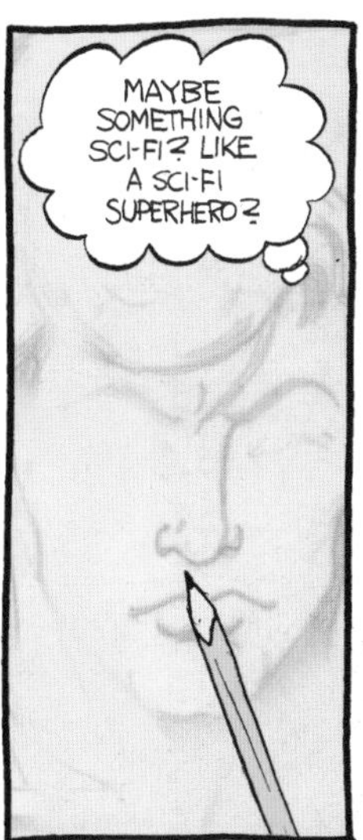
MAYBE SOMETHING SCI-FI? LIKE A SCI-FI SUPERHERO?

YEAH! THAT'S COOL. I'LL CALL HIM...

...STAR LORD! IT'S CALLED STAR LORD AND I REALLY WANT YOU TO READ IT.
COOL.
IT IS! IT'S TOTALLY COOL!
IT TAKES PLACE IN THE FUTURE, RIGHT?
AND MOST OF EARTH HAS BEEN DESTROYED BY NUCLEAR WAR.
AND STAR LORD IS THE GUY WHO IS SUPPOSED TO BE KING.
Y'KNOW, OF ALL THE PEOPLE WHO ARE STILL ALIVE.

OOOKAY?
OH!
AND HE CAN SHOOT THESE, LIKE, FIREBOLTS OUT OF THESE THINGIES ON HIS WRISTS.
PEWW! PEWW! PEWW!

UH-HUH... SO, AM I SUPPOSED TO READ THIS, OR ARE YOU JUST GONNA ACT IT OUT FOR ME?
OH, RIGHT! HA! IT'S IN MY LOCKER.

SO, WHY DO YOU WANT ME TO READ IT SO BAD?
WELL... GIRLS LIKE YOU, RIGHT?

IF YOU SAY SO...
SO, IF GIRLS LIKE YOU, AND YOU LIKE MY COMIC BOOK...
THEN, BY THE TRANSITIVE PROPERTY, IPSO FACTO, GIRLS...

... WILL LIKE ME.

WAIT! WAIT! WAIT!

ARE YOU TELLING ME THAT YOU'RE DOING A COMIC BOOK...

...TO IMPRESS GIRLS?

IN PART, YES.

WELL...

...I GUESS THERE'S A FIRST TIME FOR EVERYTHING.

THAT'S WHAT I THOUGHT!

HEY, GOOBER!

OH, HI, ELLEN!

HI!

HOW COME YOU WEREN'T AT THE MALL THIS WEEKEND?

I WAS LOOKING FOR YOU.

MY NAME'S NOT ELLEN DOLAN! IT'S ELLEN TOOLE!
SMACK!

IT IS? THEN WHY DID I THINK...
...OH! I KNOW!
ELLEN DOLAN IS THE SPIRIT's GIRLFRIEND!

WHAT TH--?!
WHO THE HECK IS "The SPIRIT"?

HE'S, LIKE, THIS CRIME FIGHTER FROM THIS OLD COMIC BOOK. IT'S A CLASSIC!

ELLEN DOLAN IS HIS GIRLFRIEND, AND SHE'S REALLY COOL! SO... UMM...
...THINKING THAT WAS YOUR NAME WAS, LIKE, A... A... COMPLIMENT!
JIMMY?

YEAH?
SHUT UP.

RRRIIIINNG
ALL RIGHT, WELL, I HAVE TO RUN TO GET TO SPANISH CLASS.

UNLIKE YOU SLACKERS...
... ELLEN TOOLE DOESN'T GET TARDY SLIPS!
BYEEE!

LATER.
SEE YA!

YOU DO REALIZE THAT SHE LIKES YOU, RIGHT?
WHAT?
NAH.., YOU'RE CRAZY!

JIMMY?
YEAH?
SHUT UP.

HEY, I'LL GIVE YOU the COMIC AFTER SCHOOL!
YOU'LL READ IT, RIGHT?
YOU'LL READ IT TONIGHT?

YES! I'LL READ IT! NOW GO TO CLASS, YOU NUT!

COOL.

THREE WEEKS!

THREE.
WEEKS.

HE DOESN'T TALK TO ME AT BASKETBALL PRACTICE.
...OR IN THE HALLS...
...OR AT LUNCH.

I TRUSTED HIM WITH MY COMIC BOOK, SOMETHING REALLY IMPORTANT!

RRRIIIING
... AND HE HASN'T EVEN BOTHERED TO READ IT.

TONY!
HEY, TONY!

HEY!
OH, HEY MAN!

DON'T GIVE ME ANY "HEY, MAN" GARBAGE.
YOU'RE AVOIDING ME.
WHAT?

NO, I'M NOT!

I'VE JUST BEEN BUSY.
OH RIGHT... "BUSY."

I ASK YOU FOR ONE FAVOR!
TO READ MY COMIC BOOK!
AND YOU CAN'T EVEN BE BOTHERED!

LOOK! I DID READ YOUR COMIC, OKAY?!
!
YOU DID?
SO...
...WHAT DID YOU THINK?
WELL...
I...
...I didn't really LIKE it.
!?...
WELL, WHO ASKED YOU?
YOU DID! (LIKE EIGHTY-FIVE TIMES!)

I'M NOT TRYING TO BE A JERK.
COULDA FOOLED ME.
LOOK, DO YOU WANNA KNOW WHAT I THINK OF YOUR DUMB COMIC BOOK, OR NOT?
NO.
FINE.
=SIGH=
GO AHEAD!
YOU SURE?
SURE.
KILL ME AND GET IT OVER WITH...

OKAY. FIRST, IT'S SUPER NERDY.
I MEAN, WHO WANTS TO READ ABOUT EVIL JEWELRY?

UMMM... HELLOOOO!
EVER HEAR OF THE LORD OF THE RINGS?
SIGH
HOW CAN I PUT THIS?

AH!
SNAP

YOU KNOW THOSE GIRLS... DAWN BRENNAN AND TAMMY MEADE?
THE CUTE PUBLIC SCHOOL GIRLS?

RIGHT.
WOULD THEY READ ABOUT EVIL SPACE JEWELRY?

OKAY, I SEE YOUR POINT.

YOU NEED AN IDEA THAT'LL REALLY GRAB PEOPLE, Y'KNOW?
SOMETHING DIFFERENT!
OH! I KNOW...
YOU SHOULD WRITE A COMIC BOOK...
...ABOUT US!
THAT'S the DUMBEST IDEA I'VE EVER HEARD!

I MEAN, IT REALLY IS.
AND WHAT DOES HE KNOW ABOUT COMICS ANYWAY?
"A COMIC BOOK ABOUT US." COME ON!
COMICS ARE ABOUT HEROES AND VILLAINS AND MUTANTS PUNCHING EACH OTHER IN THE FACE!
Y'KNOW...
BLORG!
WHAM!
...COOL STUFF.
WHO ON EARTH WOULD READ A COMIC ABOUT A COUPLE OF IDIOTS LIKE US?
GOWNLEY COMICS GROUP
1 60¢
A COUPLE OF IDIOTS
...FIRST ISSUE!
DAHR!
COLLECTOR'S ITEM...

BESIDES, I CAN'T DO SOMETHING LIKE THAT. IT'D BE WAY TOO EMBARRASSING.
BLOINK!
EXACTLY!
AT LEAST "STAR LORD" IS JUST A DUMB STORY.
NO ONE WILL THINK IT REALLY MATTERS TO YOU.
YOU HAVE SO MUCH LESS TO LOSE THAT WAY!
IF IT DOESN'T MATTER, WHY DO IT AT ALL?
IT HAS TO MATTER!
BLOINK!
BUT WHAT IF PEOPLE HATE IT?
WHAT IF THEY LAUGH AT YOU?
WHAT IF YOU'RE TOO STUPID TO REALIZE HOW DUMB THIS IDEA IS?
DON'T LISTEN TO THAT! HE'S MISSING THE WHOLE POINT!
WHICH IS?
YOU'RE A TEENAGER...

...BEING TOO STUPID TO REALIZE HOW DUMB YOU ARE IS YOUR BIGGEST ASSET!
YEAH!
BLOINK!
OKAY. I'LL GIVE IT A SHOT! WHO KNOWS? IT MIGHT EVEN BE COOL!
AND SINCE I'M JUST WRITING ABOUT MY LIFE, I BET IT'LL BE EASY!

IT'S A NIGHTMARE!

WHAT IS? YOUR COMIC BOOK?
YEAH. I'VE BEEN STUCK FOR WEEKS.

SO GO BACK TO YOUR STAR LORD IDEA IF THIS ISN'T WORKING.

NAH. THAT WAS STUPID. I JUST TOOK STAR WARS AND THE LORD OF THE RINGS AND SMOOSHED 'EM TOGETHER.

YEAH?
THAT SOUNDS PRETTY COOL.

TRUST ME, IT WASN'T...

SKITCH
SKITCH
SKITCH

SKITCH
SKITCH
SKITCH
9:35 PM

SKITCH
SKITCH
SKITCH
ERASE
ERASE
ERASE

ERASE
ERASE
ERASE
12:17 AM

SKITCH
SKITCH

SKITCH
SKITCH
2:07 AM

THE
THRILL
of
VICTORY
AND THE
AGONY
Defeat

ZZZZ
RRIIING
ACK!
HELLO? HELLO?
OH!
OH, HI!
NO... NO... I'M AWAKE.
TODAY? TO SHOOT BASKETS?
NO! NO, IT SOUNDS AWESOME!
I'LL BE RIGHT OVER!

THANKS FOR COMING, I WASN'T SURE YOU WOULD.
ELLEN! ARE YOU KIDDING? I WAS PSYCHED TO BE *INVITED!*

REALLY? YOU LOOK SORTA *TIRED.*
YEAH. I WAS KINDA UP ALL NIGHT.

YOU *WERE?* WHAT WERE YOU *DOING?*

DRAWING A COMIC BOOK.

YOU'RE **KIDDING,** RIGHT?
NO, I'M NOT **KIDDING!**
WHY WOULD I BE **KIDDING!?**

RIGHT! YOU WOULDN'T BE! *UMM...* IT SOUNDS **REALLY COOL!**
UH-**HUH**... SURE.

NO, IT IS COOL.
I LOVE THAT YOU'RE SO TALENTED.
TALENTED?
I DON'T KNOW ABOUT THAT.
WELL...
I THINK YOU'RE TALENTED.
YEAH?
YOU DO?
YEP.
HEY, LISTEN...
...I WAS WONDERING--
ELLEN!

TELEPHONE! IT'S YOUR NANA!
OKAY!

I...UHH...
...I HAVE TO TAKE THAT.
OH! Umm.. OKAY...

IT'S JUST THAT... Y'KNOW.., IT'S MY NANA.
HEY, I HAVE A NANA, TOO! GO AHEAD! IT'S FINE!

YOU SURE?
ABSOLUTELY. NANAS ARE AWESOME! TELL HER I SAID "HI."

★@#!€ NANAS!

COME ON, GOWNLEY! THIS ISN'T A BIG DEAL. JUST SAY, "WOULD YOU LIKE TO GO ON A DATE WITH ME?"

BONK!
BUT WHAT IF SHE SAYS NO?

SHE'S NOT GONNA SAY NO.

DOINK!
BUT WHAT IF SHE DOES?

THEN WE'LL JOIN A MONASTERY, AND FORGET THE WHOLE THING.
GOOD PLAN.

SORRY ABOUT THAT.
WHAT WERE YOU GONNA SAY?

WELL, I WAS JUST--
HEY, ELLEN!
OH, YOU GOTTA BE KIDDING ME!

GEEZ, WHO'S MR. GROUCHY?
OH, HEY, KRIS. THIS IS JIMMY. WE GO TO SCHOOL TOGETHER.

JIMMY, THIS IS MY NEIGHBOR KRIS.
HOW YA DOIN'?
NICE TO MEET YOU. TOO BAD YOU CAN'T STAY.

HUH? I CAN TOO STAY.
WHAT'S WRONG WITH THIS JERK?
JERK?
WHY, I--

SO, KRIS...
WHAT'S UP WITH YOU?

UGH!
WHERE DO I START?

AND SO, (approximately) TEN MILLION HOURS LATER...
...AND I HATE GEOGRAPHY.
AND I HATE SCIENCE.
AND I HATE MATH.
RIGHT.
WHO DOESN'T?
...AND IT'S NOT JUST PEANUTS! I'M ALLERGIC TO CASHEWS, AND ALMONDS
= SIGH =
THEN AGAIN, LOOK AT THE MIDDLE EAST...
UH-HUH.
YEP, SURE.
BONK BONK BONK BONK
...AND I USED THE OINTMENT
OKAY!
LOOK, ELLEN...
I'M SORRY, BUT I HAVE TO GO.
I'M EXHAUSTED.

OH... THAT'S OKAY. I HAD A GREAT TIME *ANYWAY.*
ME TOO.

SO, MAYBE WE CAN DO IT AGAIN SOME OTHER TIME.
YEAH...

...SOME OTHER TIME.

SO, MARK...
WHADDYA THINK?
THEY LOOK GREAT.
YEAH? THANKS!
YOU'VE GOT A LOT DONE, TOO.
MMM...NOT REALLY.
I STILL HAVE, LIKE, TWENTY PAGES TO GO.

HEY, MARK... THANKS FOR HANGING OUT WHILE I *DRAW*. I'M SURE IT'S NOT TOO *EXCITING*.

OH, NO! IT'S *THRILLING*!
IT'S JUST AN HONOR TO BE PRESENT AS A *MASTERPIECE* IS CREATED.

REALLY?
WOW! WELL *THANKS*, MARK! I...

THAT WAS **SARCASM**, WASN'T IT?
WHAT? OF *COURSE NOT*!

MAY I SHARPEN YOUR PENCIL, OH GREAT ONE?

THE FIRST BASKETBALL PRACTICE OF THE NEW SEASON...
HEY, TONY! CHECK IT OUT.
WHOA! COOL!
SO, IS THIS SUPPOSED TO BE US?
KINDA.
BUT, OFFICIALLY, THAT'S "PETER," AND THAT'S "FREDDY."
TO MOST PEOPLE THE FIRST DAY OF HIGH SCHOOL CAN BE A TRAUMATIC EXPERIENCE...
THE THRILL of VICTORY AND THE
I COULD NEVER DO A COMIC WHERE THE CHARACTERS WERE NAMED TONY GRAZIANO AND JIMMY GOWNLEY.
THAT WOULD JUST BE TOO WEIRD, Y'KNOW?
YEAH, I GUESS THAT WOULD BE WEIRD.
TOTALLY!

SO, ARE YOU FINISHED, YET?
NO. IT'S TAKING A LOT LONGER THAN I THOUGHT.
I WORKED ON IT ALL SUMMER BUT I STILL HAVE A BUNCH LEFT.

PLUS, I'M NEVER HAPPY WHEN I FINISH A PAGE. IT NEVER LOOKS LIKE IT DOES IN MY HEAD.

WELL, ARE THEY GETTING BETTER AS YOU GO ALONG?

ACTUALLY, I DON'T THINK SO.

AND SOMETIMES, THE HARDER I TRY, THE WORSE IT COMES OUT.

SOUNDS LIKE A LOT OF WORK FOR SUMMER VACATION. YOU MUST BE GETTING *SICK* OF IT.
I'M *NOT*, THOUGH.

I KNOW IT'S HARD WORK AND ALL, AND I'M NOT EVEN SURE IF I'M ANY *GOOD* AT IT...

...BUT, I *LOVE* IT.

IT'S KINDA HARD TO *EXPLAIN*...

...BUT, I THINK IT MIGHT BE MY *THING*, Y'KNOW?

YOUR THING?
HARVARD 00
MARIE GOT A NEW HAIRSTYLE WHICH I DIDN'T LIKE. 5 MINUTES LATER I DECIDED IT HAD GROWN ON ME
YEAH... IT'S A COMIC BOOK.
MY COMIC BOOK.
YOU DREW THIS AND YOU WROTE THE STORY?
YES.
WHEN DID YOU DO ALL OF THIS?
EVERY NIGHT FOR MONTHS.
THAT'S WHY I WANT TO PUBLISH IT.
I FIGURE IF I GET A FEW DOZEN PRINTED UP, I COULD SELL THEM TO MY FRIENDS.
AND I COULD LEARN ABOUT HOW PRINTING AND PUBLISHING WORKS.

BECAUSE THIS IS WHAT I WANT TO DO.
WHAT I WANT TO BE.
JIMMY, GIVE US A MINUTE TO TALK, OKAY?
I'M DOOMED.
THERE'S NO WAY THEY'LL GO FOR IT.
THEY PROBABLY WANT ME TO BE A DOCTOR...
...OR A LAWYER.
SOMETHING REAL. SOMETHING THAT'S NOT A CARTOONIST.
JIMMY?
YES?
HOW CAN WE HELP?

REALLY?
WOW!
THANK YOU!

THE FIRST THING WE NEED TO DO IS FIND A PRINTER.
HOW DO WE DO THAT?

I DID SOME RESEARCH.

I FIGURE ANY ONE OF 'EM SHOULD BE ABLE TO HELP.

EXECUPRINT
SORRY. THIS JOB IS TOO SMALL.

QUICK COPY
THIS JOB IS TOO BIG.

PAPPY'S PRIN
I THINK HE'S DEAD.

THIS IS AN ODD JOB FOR US. LET ME ASK OUR CAMERA GUY.
SPEEDY PRINT

MAN, WILL THIS EVER BE A PAIN. ALL THIS PENCIL, AND WASH AND JUNK...
...BUT, WHAT THE HECK, I'LL DO IT.

AWESOME! THANK YOU SO MUCH!
WHATEVER.

AND SO, ONE VERY SLOOOOOOWW MONTH LATER...
SHADES OF GRAY
NO. 0
VOL.I
$200
YOU GOT THE BOOKS!
YEP. AREN'T THEY COOL?
THEY REALLY ARE.
THEY LOOK GREAT.
THEY FEEL GREAT.
THEY EVEN SMELL GREAT.
WAIT...
HAVE YOU BEEN SITTING AROUND SNIFFING YOUR COMIC BOOK?
HEY!
DON'T KNOCK IT UNTIL YOU TRY IT.

SNIIIIIIIIIFF!

AAAAAH!!

WEIRD. THAT DOES SMELL GOOD.
SEE?

DON'T TELL ANYONE I DID THAT.
NO PROMISES.

SNIFF SNIFF
Y'KNOW WHAT THAT SMELL IS, MARK?

THE FUTURE.

SO, HAVE YOU READ IT YET?

NO, I PRETTY MUCH JUST STARE AND SNIFF.

I GUESS I'M JUST AFRAID I WON'T LIKE IT ANYMORE.

I FLIP THROUGH IT, BUT ALL I CAN SEE IS--

OH, NO!

WHAT? WHAT'S WRONG?

MOAN!
ARE YOU JUST GONNA LIE THERE, MOANING ALL NIGHT?

MOAN!
>SIGH< WELL, KNOCK IT OFF. I HAVE SOMETHING TO SHOW YOU.

WHAT DID YOU DO?
I TOOK ONE OF THE BOOKS APART.

I THOUGHT MAYBE WE COULD REARRANGE THE PAGES, AND PUT IT BACK TOGETHER.
CAN WE?
NO.

MOAN!
BUT WAIT... I NOTICED SOMETHING ELSE.

LOOK. IT'S NOT LIKE THE WHOLE BOOK IS SCREWED UP. IT'S JUST A FEW PAGES.
YES, BUT--
SHUT UP, AND LISTEN TO MY IDEA.
WHAT IF IT WAS SUPPOSED TO BE LIKE THAT? LIKE A *FLASHBACK*?
Yeah. You just add some words here to show the "flashback" is starting...
FLASHBACK?
IS THE BEST WAY TO ENSURE YOU GET ONE.
(A TALK WITH THE PRINCIPAL THAT IS)
...and some over here, to show that it's now over.
HOW DO I GET THE WORDS INTO THE BOOK?
YOU'D HAVE TO WRITE THEM IN EVERY COPY BY HAND.

OH.

JUST FORGET IT.
I QUIT.

I MESSED IT UP, IT'S RUINED, AND FIXING IT IS TOO HARD.
SO, JUST FORGET IT, OKAY?

HARD? THE WHOLE THING WAS HARD! WRITING AND DRAWING IT WAS HARD! QUITING IS STUPID!

SO QUIT WHINING AND START WRITING.

"SO, THIS IS THE FAMOUS COMIC BOOK? IT'S FINALLY FINISHED?"
"YEP. AT LONG LAST."
"IT LOOKS AMAZING! IT'S TOTALLY... WAIT A MINUTE..."

... IS THIS PART WRITTEN IN PEN?
WHAT?
NO!
WHY WOULD IT BE IN PEN?
RIGHT...
...WELL, ANYWAY, CONGRATULATIONS. I CAN'T BELIEVE YOU PUBLISHED IT!
HONESTLY, NEITHER CAN I.
SO, HOW MUCH DO I OWE YOU FOR ONE?
ARE YOU KIDDING?
NOTHING!
THE WHOLE THING WAS YOUR IDEA.
OH, COME ON!
I DON'T KNOW ABOUT THAT!
REALLY... THANKS FOR EVERYTHING. IT MEANS A LOT.
OH, SHUT UP, YOU FREAKIN' WEIRDO.

HEY, GUYS! WHAT'S UP?

ELLEN! CHECK IT OUT!

HEY! YOU FINALLY FINISHED THE COMIC!

CONGRATULATIONS!

THANKS!

YOU..

...YOU CAN KEEP IT IF YOU WANT.

WHAT? OH, NO! LET ME BUY IT! HOW MUCH *ARE* THEY?

NOTHING! FORGET IT!

TONY, HOW MUCH ARE THEY?

LOOKS LIKE TWO DOLLARS.

JIMMY!

I CAN *PAY* TWO DOLLARS!

I KNOW YOU CAN..
I JUST.. I...
... I WANT TO GIVE IT TO YOU...
...AS A GIFT!
AWW! WELL, THANKS!
I CAN'T WAIT TO READ IT!
FLIP FLIP FLIP
SO, HAVE YOU SOLD MANY YET?
UMM... JUST YOU TWO SO FAR.
SO...
...NONE?
TECHNICALLY, YEAH... NONE.

ELLEN! DO YOU KNOW IF WE HAVE A--
UHH... WHAT ARE YOU GUYS LOOKING AT?

JIMMY'S COMIC BOOK! HE DREW IT *HIMSELF*.
IT'S *REALLY COOL*. YOU SHOULD BUY ONE.

HOW MUCH IS IT?
UHH.. WELL, I DON'T--
IT'S TWO DOLLARS!

HEH HEH
IT'S... UHH... TWO DOLLARS.

COOL. HERE YA GO!
THANKS!

MY FIRST SALE!
IT FEELS...
...WEIRD!

WELL, GET USED TO IT. I'M SURE IT'S THE FIRST OF MANY.
AND HEY, YOU CAN USE THE MONEY FOR THE MOVIE TONIGHT! PERFECT TIMING!

SEE YOU THEN, OKAY?
YEP! see YA THEN!

SO... ANOTHER "NOT-A-DATE" DATE?
YEAH. I THINK THIS IS NUMBER FOUR.

WILL YOU JUST ASK HER TO BE YOUR GIRLFRIEND ALREADY?
THIS IS GETTING OLD!

LOOK, I PROMISE I HAVE EVERY INTENTION OF ASKING HER TONIGHT!
I'M DETERMINED!
I'M CONFIDENT!

"...SO THERE'S LIKE A ONE IN TEN CHANCE I'LL GO THROUGH WITH IT."
MALL-WIDE SALE
ALL THIS WEEKEND
SCHUYLKILL MALL
the movies
GANGSTER DAYS
BABY TALK
FAMILY TREE
TIME WARP PART 2
GIFT CARDS AVAILABLE

WILL YOU BE MY GIRLFRIEND?
WILL YOU BE MY GIRLFRIEND?
WILL YOU BE MY GIRLFRIEND.

WILL...

YOU MADE IT!
BARELY! IT'S REALLY COMING DOWN OUT THERE.

WOW! YOUR HAIR IS SO FANCY.
OH! YEAH...

MY NANA DID IT FOR ME.
DO YOU LIKE IT?

YEAH! IT LOOKS REALLY COOL.
THANKS. GOTTA LOVE THOSE NANAS, RIGHT?
HA HA HA! YEP.
SO, DO YOU WANNA GET SOMETHING TO EAT FIRST?
SURE.

LET'S GO TO McDONALD'S. MY FRIEND LYNN IS WORKING.
SHE PROBABLY WON'T CHARGE US.
NOW YOU'RE TALKIN'!

HAVE YOU EVER NOTICED HOW THERE ARE ONLY, LIKE, FOUR DIFFERENT McNUGGET SHAPES?
AND CHECK THIS OUT...

I KNOW! AND NONE OF THEM ARE SUPER APPETIZING!
THIS ONE LOOKS LIKE A HUMAN KIDNEY!
TWO REGULAR NUGGETS FUSED INTO ONE GIGANTIC MEGA-NUGGET.
THAT IS COMPLETELY DISGUSTING.

EEEEW! GROSS!
DISGUSTING? I THINK IT'S ROMANTIC.
OH, YOU DO, HUH?

TOTALLY! TWO INDIVIDUAL LUMPS OF MEAT, JOINED FOREVER BY THE ACT OF DEEP FRYING. WHAT COULD BE MORE TOUCHING?
YOU HAVE TO SHARE IT WITH ME!
WHAT? NO! GET OUT OF HERE!
C'MON, IT'LL BE A TOTAL "DEAR DIARY" MOMENT.
HAHAHA
SIGH
OKAY, YOU WEIRDO.
LIKE THIS?
YEP. JUST PULL IT AND...
SPLEWCH
YUCK.
OKAY. YEAH. THAT WAS GROSS.

WILL YOU BE MY GIRLFRIEND?
YES!

YOU WILL?!

ABSOLUTELY!

WOW.

MAY I ASK WHY?

SIGH
YOU ARE SUCH A GOOBER.
THE GOOBIEST!

movies
GANGSTER DAYS
FAMILY
SO...
...WHAT DO YOU WANT TO SEE?
DOESN'T MATTER.
WANT A PEPPERMINT?
NO THANKS.
UGH. THE ONLY MOVIE PLAYING IS GANGSTER DAYS. NOT REALLY OUR SCENE.
TWO FOR GANGSTER DAYS, PLEASE.

JIMMY, YOU DON'T SERIOUSLY WANT TO SIT AND WATCH GANGSTER DAYS, DO YOU?
NOPE.
oOOKAY...
...WELL, THEN WHY...!
OH!
Umm... ON SECOND THOUGHT...

...I THINK I WILL TAKE THAT MINT.
COMING SOON
First Kisses

SO, MY MOM READ YOUR COMIC BOOK LAST NIGHT.
SHE DID?
YEP.
SHE LIKED IT A LOT.
...BUT SHE SAID THAT YOUR NAME WAS ON IT SO MANY TIMES THAT YOU MUST BE AN EGOMANIAC.
SHE REALLY SAID THAT?
YEPPERS.
WELL...
...SHE'S PROBABLY NOT WRONG.
HEE HEE
SERIOUSLY, SHE REALLY DID LIKE IT. SHE ASKED IF YOU'RE GONNA MAKE A SECOND ONE.
I ALREADY STARTED A SECOND ONE.
THIRD. ACTUALLY.
(NOT COUNTING THIS STUPID STAR LORD THING I TRIED.)

THIRD?

UH-HUH. I NEVER REALLY TOLD ANYONE, BUT I MADE A COMIC WHEN I WAS A LITTLE KID.

ACTUALLY, I ALMOST FORGOT ABOUT IT.
I MADE IT AS A PRESENT FOR MARNIE MARQUARDT.

HUH?
WHAT'S A "MARNIE MARQUARDT"?

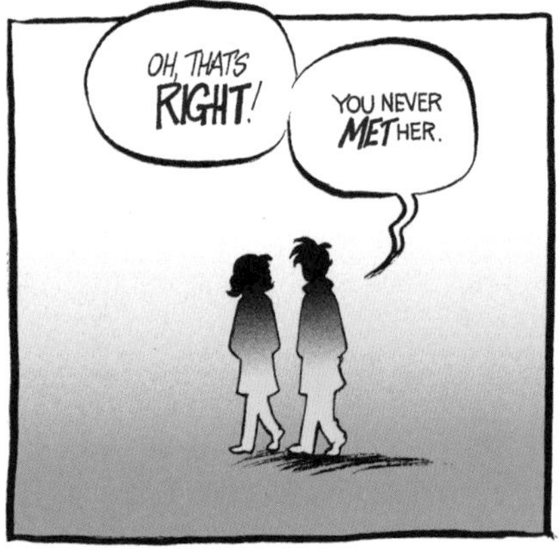
OH, THAT'S RIGHT!
YOU NEVER MET HER.

Marnie Marquardt

WAS THE TOMBOY WHO LIVED UP THE STREET FROM ME.

SHE WAS COOL. SHE WAS FUNNY. AND WE LIKED THE SAME THINGS. SHE EVEN LIKED **STAR WARS** ENOUGH TO FORM A JEDI KNIGHT CLUB WITH ME, AND WE DEFENDED THE STREETS OF GIRARDVILLE FROM EVIL SITH LORDS...

TASTE JEDI JUSTICE!

"JEDI" ME!

YAGH!

"JEDI" MARNIE!

SUSPECTED "SITH"!

...WHICH, TO THE UNTRAINED EYE, MAY HAVE APPEARED LIKE TWO WEIRD KIDS IN BATHROBES SWINGING WIFFLE BALL BATS.

EAT "the FORCE," you SITH DIRTBAG!
ACTUAL ME!
WHAT is WRONG WITH YOU WEIRDOS?!
ACTUAL MARNIE!
THE CLUB ONLY LASTED AN AFTERNOON, BUT FOR FOUR YEARS WE WERE INSEPARABLE.
RANDOM NEIGHBORHOOD IDIOT!

AND I ADORED HER.

MAN, I CAN'T BELIEVE SUMMER IS HALF OVER. WE'LL BE BACK IN SCHOOL SOON.
YEAH. I GUESS SO.

I WONDER IF OUR LUNCH TABLES WILL BE CLOSE TO EACH OTHER? OR IF WE'LL HAVE RECESS TOGETHER? AND DO YOU THINK–

LOOK! I DON'T KNOW, ALL RIGHT?
WILL YOU JUST SHUT UP ABOUT IT?!
OKAY! OKAY!
GEEZ, WHAT'S YOUR PROBLEM?

I'M SORRY, I.. LOOK, CAN WE JUST NOT TALK ABOUT SCHOOL?

OH.. UH.. YEAH..
..YEAH, SURE!

HOW IS MARNIE DOING?
OKAY, I GUESS, BUT KINDA GRUMPY.

I GUESS SHE HAS A LOT ON HER MIND.
SHE DOES? WHY?

WELL, GETTING READY TO MOVE AWAY AND ALL...

MOVE AWAY?!

SHE...
...SHE DIDN'T TELL YOU?

EXCUSE ME.
I DON'T FEEL VERY GOOD.

...BUT EVEN AFTER I FOUND OUT, WE JUST *IGNORED* THE WHOLE THING.
MARNIE KNEW THAT I KNEW AND ALL...
...BUT NEITHER ONE OF US TALKED ABOUT IT.
IT'S ALMOST DARK.
I GOTTA GET GOING.
I WAS HAVING SO MUCH FUN. I WISH I COULD STAY.
me too.
THE DAY BEFORE SHE LEFT, SHE GAVE ME A BIG STACK OF BASEBALL CARDS AS A GOOD-BYE PRESENT.
I GAVE HER NOTHING.

BUT LATER...
...ALONE IN MY SPIDER-MAN UNDEROOS...
..I CONTEMPLATED A MARNIELESS EXISTENCE.

UNDEROOS?

I KNEW I COULDN'T STOP HER FROM LEAVING...

...BUT I AT LEAST WANTED HER TO KNOW HOW I FELT.

SO, I DECIDED TO MAKE HER A COMIC BOOK. IT COULDN'T HAVE BEEN MORE THAN A FEW PAGES LONG, AND I DON'T EVEN REMEMBER WHAT IT WAS ABOUT...

...BUT I DO REMEBER WHAT IT WAS CALLED.

MARNIE RULES!

BY JIMMY

DON'T BE GONE.
PLEASE, PLEASE, PLEASE! DON'T BE GONE.

MARNIE RULES!
M

IT WAS TOO LATE.

MARNIE RULES!
BY JIMMY

MARNIE RULES!
BY JIMMY

MARNIE RULES
BY JIMMY

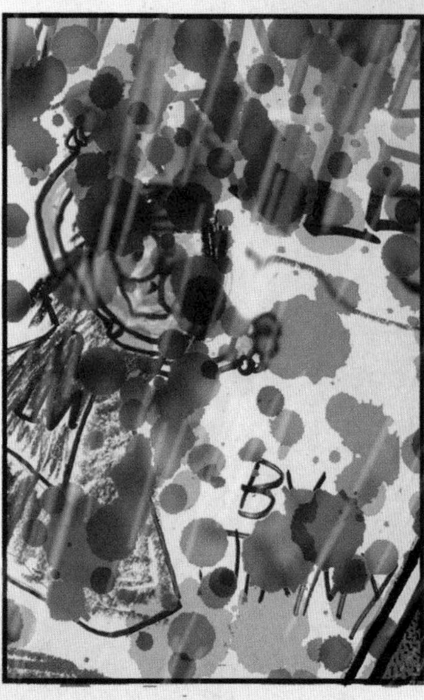

SO, SHE NEVER EVEN GOT TO SEE IT?
NO.

THAT'S SO SAD!
YOU LIKED HER A LOT, DIDN'T YOU?

YEAH. SHE WAS ONE OF MY BEST FRIENDS. I STILL MISS HER.
I CAN TELL.

JIMMY? I HAVE A CONFESSION.
WHAT'S THAT?

I HATE MARNIE MARQUARDT.

IT'S SO COOL THAT YOUR MOM OWNS A VIDEO STORE.
OH, WE ARE LIVING THE DREAM, ALL RIGHT.
ANYWAY, MY MOM AND SISTER HAVE A SURPRISE FOR YOU.

REALLY? WHAT--
WHOA!

r Mike's Video
TA-DA!
ON SALE!

WE GOT A BUNCH OF COPIES FROM YOUR MOM THAT WE WANT YOU TO SIGN, AND TRACY HAS ANOTHER SURPRISE FOR YOU.
TRACY! SHOW HIM.

I MADE 'EM IN SHOP CLASS.
WOW!
SHADES GRAY

I CAN MAKE MORE, TOO. I FIGURED WE COULD SELL THEM.
OH, MY GOD! I HAVE MERCH! THANK YOU SO MUCH!

SIGNING BOOKS IS KINDA WEIRD!
BOY, YOU HAVE SLOPPY HANDWRITING.

ON THE OTHER HAND...

...WITH A LITTLE PRACTICE...

...I THINK I CAN GET USED TO IT.

JIMMY!
JIMMY, WAIT!

OH, HI... UH... STEVE, RIGHT?
THAT'S RIGHT.
I WANNA BUY A COMIC BOOK.
I DIDN'T HAVE THE MONEY BEFORE, BUT I DO NOW.
OKAY, GREAT!
THEY'RE TWO DOLLARS.
TWO?
OH, I THOUGHT IT WAS JUST ONE.
I'LL HAVE TO GET IT SOME OTHER TIME.
UMM... LOOK, STEVE... JUST TAKE IT, OKAY? ON THE HOUSE.
ARE YOU SURE?
YEAH. JUST DO ME A FAVOR, AND TALK IT UP, OKAY? WE'LL CALL IT ADVERTISING.
OKAY! I WILL, THANKS!

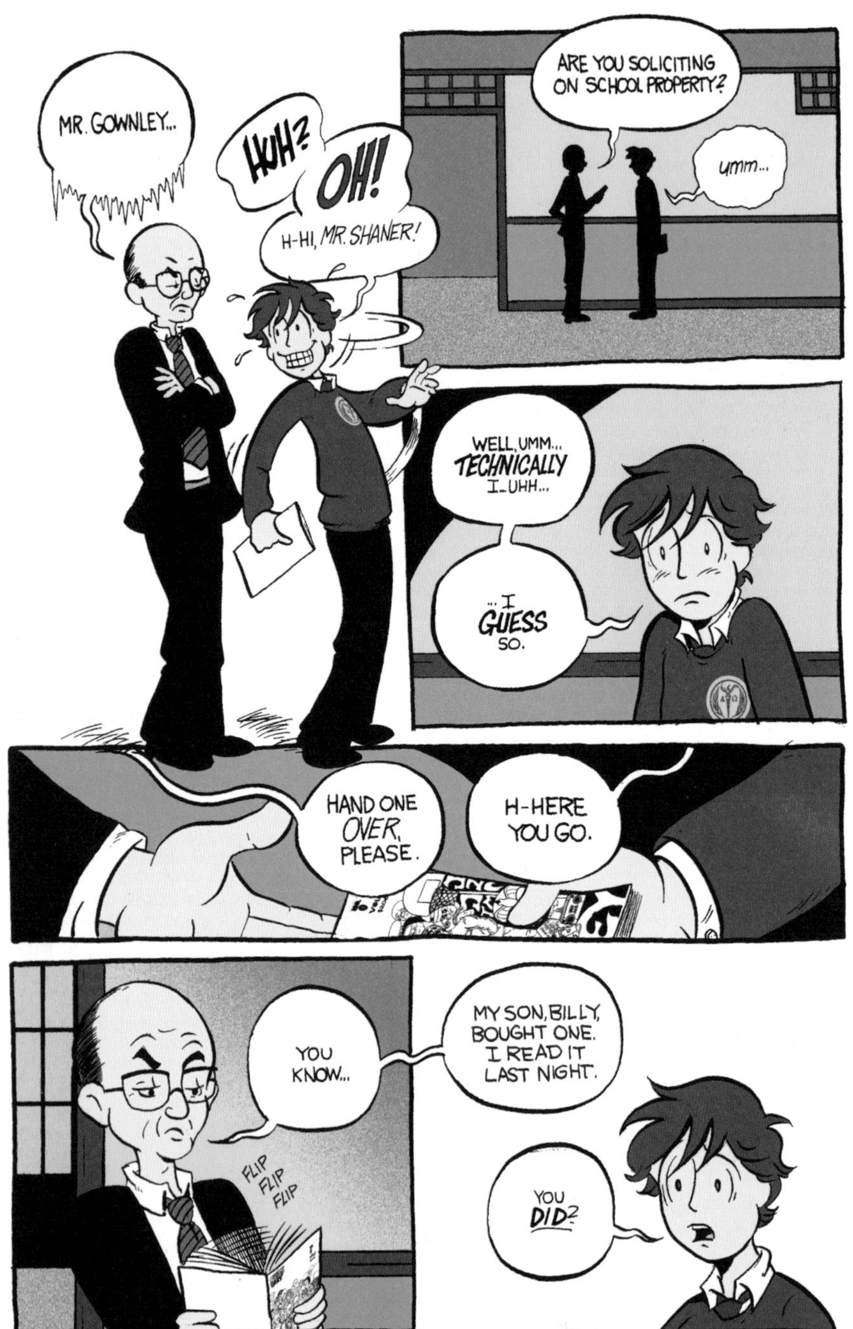
MR. GOWNLEY...
HUH? OH!
H-HI, MR. SHANER!
ARE YOU SOLICITING ON SCHOOL PROPERTY?
umm...
WELL, UMM... TECHNICALLY I...UHH...
...I GUESS SO.
HAND ONE OVER, PLEASE.
H-HERE YOU GO.
YOU KNOW...
MY SON, BILLY, BOUGHT ONE. I READ IT LAST NIGHT.
FLIP FLIP FLIP
YOU DID?

I DID, AND I LIKED IT A LOT.
I THOUGHT IT WAS VERY FUNNY.

THANKS! I WORKED REALLY HARD ON IT.
WELL, IT SHOWS.

THAT KID... STEVE... THE ONE YOU JUST GAVE THE BOOK TO.

YOU KNOW HIS FAMILY DOESN'T HAVE TWO NICKELS TO RUB TOGETHER, *RIGHT?*

YEAH.
YEAH, I KNOW.

WELL, IT'S GOOD TO KNOW THAT IN TWENTY YEARS OF TEACHING, I TAUGHT ONE OR TWO NICE KIDS.
TRY NOT TO BECOME A JERK.

I WONDER WHAT MADE HIM SAY *THAT?*

ERT!

CONGRATULATIONS
JIMMY...
Shades of Gray
COMICS AND STORIES
OUR CELEBRITY!!!

WHEN DID **THIS** GO UP?
JUST NOW. THE GUIDANCE COUNSELOR DID IT.

YES, MISTER GOWNLEY, YOU'VE BEEN MAKING QUITE THE IMPRESSION LATELY.
OH!
UMM... HI, SISTER REGINA ALMA!
YES! I...I GUESS SO!

WELL, YOU DO HAVE A TALENT... SUCH AS IT IS... AND YOU FOUND A WAY TO USE IT.

THAT'S MORE THAN MOST PEOPLE CAN SAY.

NICE JOB.

THANK YOU, SISTER!

WHAT IS HAPPENING?

THEN... ON TOP OF *THAT*...

DO YOU EVER FEEL LIKE YOU LIVE ON THE WRONG PLANET?
ONLY EVERY DAY.
LISTEN, I NEED TO TALK TO YOU ABOUT SOMETHING.

WELL, A FEW TEACHERS HAVE APPROACHED THE STUDEN COUNCIL ABOUT HAVING A SPECIAL DAY CELEBRATING YOUR COMIC BOOK.
REALLY?

YEAH. HOW DOES THAT SOUND?
GREAT!

UHH... GOOD... UM... WE THOUGHT THAT MAYBE YOU COULD GIVE A PRESENTATION AND...
UH-HUH!

OH, BOY!

... SO, TELL ME ...
... WHERE DO YOU GET YOUR *IDEAS?*
16 WKSA
THE NEWS CHANNEL
16 WKSA

OH! UMM... WELL...

THAT'S A GOOD QUESTION.
I DON'T KNOW REALLY.

It's just stuff that I notice, or stuff that I think about sometimes. Stuff that I find funny or interesting.

DO YOU FEEL THAT YOUR WORK HAS A MESSAGE?

Well, I guess...hmmm...I guess if people read the book and think about the things the characters go through...

...maybe they'd realize that the things kids think about or experience are serious, y'know? Or at least they are to kids...

"I THINK SOMETIMES ADULTS FORGET THAT."
SAW YOU ON TV!
YOU DID GREAT!
WERE YOU NERVOUS?
I BOUGHT A COMIC FOR MY NIECE.
GREAT TO SEE A LOCAL KID MAKE GOOD.
YOU'RE SO TALENTED.
NOW, ARE YA GONNA WIN THIS GAME TONIGHT?
WELL, IT DOES FEEL GOOD HAVING THE HOME COURT ADVANTAGE.

HEY THERE BIG STAR!
HA! WELL, YOU KNOW HOW IT IS.
YOU LOOKED VERY CUTE ON TV. I'M PROUD OF YOU.
THANKS!

NOW, IF YOU'LL EXCUSE ME, WE HAVE A GAME SO I NEED TO GO AND EXCEL AT YET ANOTHER THING.
-SIGH-
THEY'VE CREATED A MONSTER.

SPARTANS 7
CHARG 21
SPARTANS 5
BZZZZZZZZZZZZZZZ
CHARGERS 21
CHARG 33
CHARGERS 42

DID YOU SEE THAT?
WHAT A GAME!
HUH? WHY ARE YOU SO HAPPY?
WHAT DO YOU MEAN? I SCORED 27 POINTS. A PERSONAL BEST.
YEAH, THERE'S JUST ONE PROBLEM...
...YOU WERE ON THE LOSING TEAM, GOOBER.
73 84
HOME PERIOD AWAY
OH...UHH...
SO, YOU WANNA GO GET A CHEESEBURGER? MAYBE YOU CAN EXCEL AT THAT.
YOU'RE HILARIOUS, Y'KNOW THAT?
THANKS! MAYBE I SHOULD WRITE A COMIC BOOK, TOO.

HEY, DID YOU GUYS SEE THE NEWSPAPER THIS SATURDAY?
NOPE.

WELL, CHECK IT OUT! A HUGE ARTICLE ABOUT YOURS TRULY.

WOW.
COOL.
TEEN CARTOONIST

YEAH, I GUESS THEY WANTED TO BOOST THE OL' CIRCULATION, SO THEY FEATURED *ME*.
HEH HEH

HEY, JIMMY... IS THAT YOU IN THE PAPER?
DUH, EINSTEIN.

IT'S AN ARTICLE ABOUT MY COMIC.
OH YEAH. I READ YOUR BOOK, BUT I DIDN'T REALLY GET IT.

I'M NOT SURPRISED. YOU'RE KIND OF AN IDIOT.
DROP DEAD, JERK!
BACK ATYA, LOSER!

SO! HOW ABOUT THAT GAME ON FRIDAY? WAS THAT SOMETHING OR WHAT?

WE LOST.
BADLY.

MAN! WHY IS EVERYONE SO HUNG UP ON THAT?

SO, MY SECOND COMIC WILL BE COMING OUT SOON.
DO YOU THINK I SHOULD START CHARGING FOR AUTOGRAPHS?

OH, DON'T WORRY...I'LL GIVE TEAMMATES A DISCOUNT.

LATER...
HEY, TONY...
=SIGH=
WHAT NOW?
I WAS THINKING ABOUT THE WHOLE COMIC BOOK DAY THING, DO YOU--
THERE'S NOT GONNA BE A COMIC BOOK DAY!
I KILLED IT!
I DON'T THINK ANYONE CAN STAND ANY MORE OF THE JIMMY GOWNLEY SHOW.
YOU WHAT?
MAYBE IT'S NOT JUST ABOUT ME, HUH? MAYBE MY COMIC GOT ATTENTION BECAUSE SOMETHING COOL FINALLY CAME OUT OF THIS DUMP!
WHATEVER, MAN...
...I HOPE YOU'RE HAVING FUN.

SIGH
GOOOOOOD MORNING
POKE POKE
OH...
...HI.
GEEZ! WHAT'S WRONG WITH YOU?
NOTHING. I'M JUST IN A BAD MOOD, I GUESS.
BAD MOOD, HUH?
SO, WHAT, ARE WE GONNA BE MR. GRUMPY PANTS ALL DAY NOW?

YES! MAYBE I AM! MAYBE I'M GOING TO BE "MR. GRUMPY PANTS" ALL DAY! IS THAT ALLOWED?!

NO.

NOW, COME HERE AND *LOOK!*
?!

TA-DA!
SPRING TRIP to NEW YORK CITY!
April 14th
April 14th
See a Broadway Show!
See Sister Patricia Mary for details

WHAT? THE *NEW YORK* TRIP? WHO *CARES*? THEY DO IT *EVERY YEAR*.

YEAH...BUT *THIS* YEAR, **WE** ARE GOING **TOGETHER**.

ELLEN, C'MON! IT'S JUST *WAY* TOO *EXPENSIVE*. I'D HAVE TO PAY FOR THE *BUS*, AND BUY A TICKET FOR THE *SHOW*...

...*PLUS*, THERE ARE ALL OF THE *MEALS* AND STUFF...IT'S JUST *TOO MUCH*.

NOT A *PROBLEM*.

MY DAD IS PAYING FOR THE *WHOLE TRIP* FOR ME AND A FRIEND OF MY *CHOOSING*...

...AND I'M CHOOSING **YOU**, FRIEND OF *MINE*.

ACTUALLY, IT'S QUITE EASY. LOOK AT ME NOT BEING IN NEW YORK **RIGHT NOW**.

FOR MY NEXT TRICK, I WON'T BE IN KENTUCKY.

=SIGH=
JIMMY, SHUT UP.

SERIOUSLY, THIS IS SO COOL. TELL YOUR DAD THANKS.

OKAY, I WILL.

AND BECAUSE WE GET TO THE CITY EARLY, WE'LL HAVE TIME TO SIGHTSEE.

THERE'S JUST ONE SMALL DOWNSIDE...

BEEP! BEEP! BEEP!
5:00 AM

SLEEPY, HUH?
Y'KNOW, I GET UP EVERY DAY AT THIS TIME.

WELL, THAT SUCKS.

AHH...
YA GET USED TO IT.

HI, MRS. GOWNLEY.
HELLO, ELLEN.

YOU KIDS HAVE FUN TODAY.
WE WILL.

AND BE CAREFUL!

STICK TOGETHER, AND DON'T
WANDER INTO ANY DANGEROUS
AND DON'T
AND BE
YOU DON'T FORGET
SHE TENDS TO WORRY.
AWW...
...I THINK IT'S SWEET.

AND SO, ONE THREE-HOUR BUS RIDE LATER...
ZZZZ

JIMMY! JIMMY!

WAKE UP.

WE'RE HERE.

WOW!

WELL, STUDENTS, PAY ATTENTION.
THIS IS NOT GIRARDVILLE, PA. THIS IS NEW YORK CITY. SO PLEASE BE CAREFUL.
NO ONE IS TO WANDER OFF ALONE.
ALWAYS TRAVEL WITH AT LEAST ONE OTHER PERSON.
AND REMEMBER TO RETURN TO THIS SPOT IMMEDIATELY AFTER YOUR SHOW.
YOU DON'T WANT THE BUS TO LEAVE WITHOUT YOU.
NOW, WE HAVE A FEW HOURS UNTIL SHOWTIME, SO YOU ARE FREE TO...
...EXPLORE!
PTWANG!

VISIT Kappy's GRILL
Broadway's Hottest SHOW!
MOON FEVER
ERIC'S
Stellanna's

WOW. THE METROPOLITAN MUSEUM OF ART!
THIS IS AMAZING!
I MEAN JUST THE BUILDING IS AMAZING.
HUH? OH, I KNOW. IT REALLY IS.
LET'S SEE...
AH! 900. THAT'S WHERE THE MONETS ARE.
I WANNA GO THERE FIRST.
HE'S MY FAVORITE.
I HAVE TWO POSTERS OF HIS IN MY ROOM.
C'MON!
THIS WAY!

WOW.
ISN'T IT GORGEOUS!?
YEAH!
IT... IT REALLY IS!

I MEAN, WHEN YOU *FIRST LOOK*, IT'S JUST A RANDOM MESS OF PAINT.

BUT AFTER A WHILE, IT ALL SEEMS SO *REAL*.
REALER THAN REAL!
LIKE YOU'RE JUST LOOKING THROUGH A WINDOW, Y'KNOW?

LIKE YOU CAN STEP RIGHT IN!
THIS IS AWESOME.
I'VE NEVER SEEN ANYTHING LIKE IT.

AND THOSE COMICS I MADE...
...I CAN'T BELIEVE I THOUGHT THEY WERE GOOD.
I CHARGED **MONEY** FOR THEM!
THAT'S JUST **HUMILIATING.**

WHOA!
LOOK AT THAT!

VASE OF IRISES
BY VINCENT
VAN GOGH.

IT'S PRETTY.
UH-HUH.

BUT I'VE NEVER BEEN A BIG FAN OF HIS, Y'KNOW?
YOU CAN SEE EVERY BRUSH-STROKE.

AND THE WHOLE EAR THING? I MEAN GROSS!
HE WAS JUST SOME GUY, BUT HE DID THIS!

WHAT DO YOU... UHH... JIMMY?
IT STILL LOOKS WET!

JIMMY!
TOUCH!

...ZZZZZZ..

HUH?

ACK!

PUFF
PUFF
PUFF
WHEW!
HAHAHA
HAHAHA
HAHAHA
HAHAHA
HAHAHA
HAHAHA
HAHAHA
HAHAHA

IT WAS AMAZING!

THE SHOW!
THE CITY!
EVERYTHING!

AND WE WENT TO THIS MUSEUM, Y'KNOW? THE BIG ONE? AND WE SAW ALL THESE PAINTINGS.
REAL PICASSOS! REAL MONETS!

IT WAS... I MEAN... I'VE SEEN PICTURES, BUT YOU CAN'T UNDERSTAND UNTIL YOU JUST CAN'T!
I...

ARE YOU OKAY? YOU'RE GETTING VERY WORKED UP.
SORRY, I... I'M JUST TIRED!

I THINK I'M JUST GONNA GO UP TO MY ROOM.
I KINDA NEED TO BE ALONE...

I HAVE A LOT TO THINK ABOUT.

SO, ELLEN...
WILL YOU GO TO THE *PROM* WITH ME?
OF COURSE!

I HAVE TO ADMIT, I THOUGHT YOU *FORGOT* ABOUT IT.
HONESTLY?

MY *MOM* HAD TO REMIND ME.
=SIGH=
JIMMY? FOR YOUR OWN SAKE...

...DON'T TELL ANYONE ELSE THAT PART.

SAY CHEESE!
CLICK

CUTE DATE!

WHY IS SHE WITH YOU?
WELL, THERE'S NO ACCOUNTING FOR *TASTE*.

HEY, LISTEN... I JUST WANTED TO SAY THAT I WAS SORRY.
HUH?
FOR *WHAT*?

FOR CANCELING YOUR BIG DAY. I SHOULDN'T HAVE DONE THAT.

AH, DON'T WORRY ABOUT IT.
IT WAS PROBABLY FOR THE BEST, ANYWAY.
THINGS WERE GETTING A LITTLE OUT OF HAND.
YEAH, MAYBE A LITTLE.
CHARGING FOR AUTOGRAPHS! SHEESH
HEY! I SAID YOU'D GET A DISCOUNT!
HA!
WHOOPS! 'SCUSE ME. I'M GOING TO DANCE WITH MY DATE NOW.
FINE! GO AHEAD... I HOPE YOU'RE HAVING FUN.
Y'KNOW WHAT?
I THINK I AM.

...AND DOWN THERE WAS WHERE WE PLAYED BASKETBALL, AND RIGHT UP THERE WAS WHERE MARNIE LIVED.
UGH! YOU MEAN YOUR LITTLE GIRLFRIEND?

SHE WAS NOT MY GIRLFRIEND!
WE WERE LITTLE KIDS!
YEAH YEAH YEAH.

THE AMUSEMENT PARK WAS FUN TODAY, WASN'T IT?
IT WAS! IT WAS ALL FUN.

IT WAS THE PERFECT PROM WEEKEND.

BUT IT'S LATE.

SO, DO YOU NEED TO GO HOME NOW?
WELL...NOT YET. LET'S GO FOR A WALK.
THE NIGHT IS SO BEAUTIFUL.
On certain nights, when the sky was clear, and a soft breeze tickled the hair on the back of my neck, and the coal dust landscape melded with the deep black of the rural night sky...
...I could be fooled into thinking that I was living in the most beautiful place on earth...
...and that the summers of my youth were the best of all possible summers.
DID YOU JUST COME UP WITH THAT?
NAH. IT'S FROM MY NEXT COMIC, AND IT TOOK ME, LIKE, THREE WEEKS JUST TO WRITE THAT ONE PART.
AT THAT RATE, I WON'T FINISH UNTIL I'M 40.
WELL, IT'S WONDERFUL.

AND IT'S PRETTY SWEET AND SENTIMENTAL. I DIDN'T KNOW YOU FELT THAT WAY ABOUT GOOD OL' GIRARDVILLE.
I DIDN'T, Y'KNOW? BUT NEW YORK CHANGED THINGS FOR ME.
IT DID?

YEAH. SEEING ALL OF THOSE ARTISTS, THOSE GENIUSES, I REALIZED SOMETHING...
...I HAVE NO TALENT WHATSOEVER!

JIMMY! THAT'S NOT TRUE!
NO, IT IS! AND I'M OKAY WITH IT!

LOOK, IF I WAS A KID IN NEW YORK, OR L.A., NO ONE WOULD HAVE CARED ABOUT MY DUMB COMICS.
I WOULDN'T HAVE BEEN ON TV, OR IN THE PAPER.

JIFFY MART
THE ONLY REASON, THOSE BOOKS WERE SPECIAL, WAS BECAUSE EVERYONE BELIEVED THEY WERE SPECIAL.
BELIEVED I WAS SPECIAL.

NOW, I JUST NEED TO PROVE THEM RIGHT.
SO, I THREW OUT THE COMIC I WAS WORKING ON BEFORE NEW YORK.
I STARTED ON SOMETHING NEW, AND I'M GONNA WORK AND WORK TILL IT'S PERFECT.
WILL YOU SHOW IT TO ME?
SURE! YOU WANT TO GO SEE IT NOW?
IN A MINUTE. I NEED TO SAY SOMETHING FIRST.
LOOK, JIMMY, I NEED YOU TO PROMISE ME SOMETHING...
...YOU'RE AN ARTIST.
YOU SEE THINGS DIFFERENTLY THAN ANYONE I KNOW.
NO MATTER WHAT HAPPENS, YOU HAVE TO PROMISE YOU WON'T STOP BEING AN ARTIST, OKAY? IT'S REALLY IMPORTANT.
WHAT DO YOU MEAN... "NO MATTER--"
YOU HAVE TO PROMISE!

OKAY. OKAY. I PROMISE...
...YOU WEIRDO.
ANYTHING ELSE?
WELL...

...THERE IS JUST ONE...
...LITTLE...
...THING.

HAVE A PEPPERMINT.

UMM...
...OKAY, I...

WHY MISS TOOLE! I AM SHOCKED! SHOCKED! IS THIS ANY WAY FOR A PROPER YOUNG LADY TO BEHAVE?!
SIGH

JIMMY?
YEAH?

SHUT UP.

YOU BROKE UP?!
SCHUYLKILL MALL
CO E VISIT
OUR FAM LY
OF ST RES
O

YEAH. WE BROKE UP.
WAIT. DID YOU BREAK UP WITH HER?

NO.

SO, SHE BROKE UP WITH YOU?

OBVIOUSLY.

WOW.
I DID NOT SEE THAT COMING.

WELL, TONY...
...REAL LIFE DOESN'T HAVE FORESHADOWING.

SO, WHAT HAPPENED?
I DON'T KNOW.

HOW CAN YOU NOT KNOW?
I DON'T WANT TO TALK ABOUT IT.

WAIT. YOU DON'T WANT TO TALK ABOUT HOW YOU DON'T KNOW WHAT HAPPENED, OR YOU DO KNOW WHAT HAPPENED, AND YOU DON'T WANT TO TALK ABOUT THAT?

WE...
WE STARTED ARGUING A LITTLE... THEN WE STARTED ARGUING A LOT.
THEN WE HAD ONE BIG ARGUMENT.

AND THAT WAS IT?
THAT WAS IT.

WELL, LOOK... I... UMM...
...WHAT?
OH.
LET'S...
...LET'S JUST GO, OKAY?

LOOK, FORGET ABOUT THAT. THERE ARE LOTS OF GIRLS.
JUST WORK ON GETTING YOUR NEXT COMIC DONE.

I-I *CAN'T.* THERE WAS AN ACCIDENT. I LEFT A GLASS OF WATER LYING AROUND.

IT GOT SPILLED ON THE PAGES. IT RUINED EVERY SINGLE ONE.

ALL THAT WORK, AND IT JUST WASHED AWAY LIKE IT NEVER HAPPENED AT ALL.

OKAY, THAT STINKS, BUT SO WHAT, RIGHT?
YOU CAN REDO IT.
MAYBE EVERYTHING GETS WASHED AWAY EVENTUALLY.

RIGHT! IT'LL BE EVEN BETTER THIS TIME.
MAYBE EVERYTHING... FRIENDS... ART... LOVE... MAYBE IT ALL JUST FADES AWAY.

SURE! ALL IT TAKES IS A LITTLE... UH... A LITTLE...
BUT...
...THEN WHAT?

...JIMMY?!

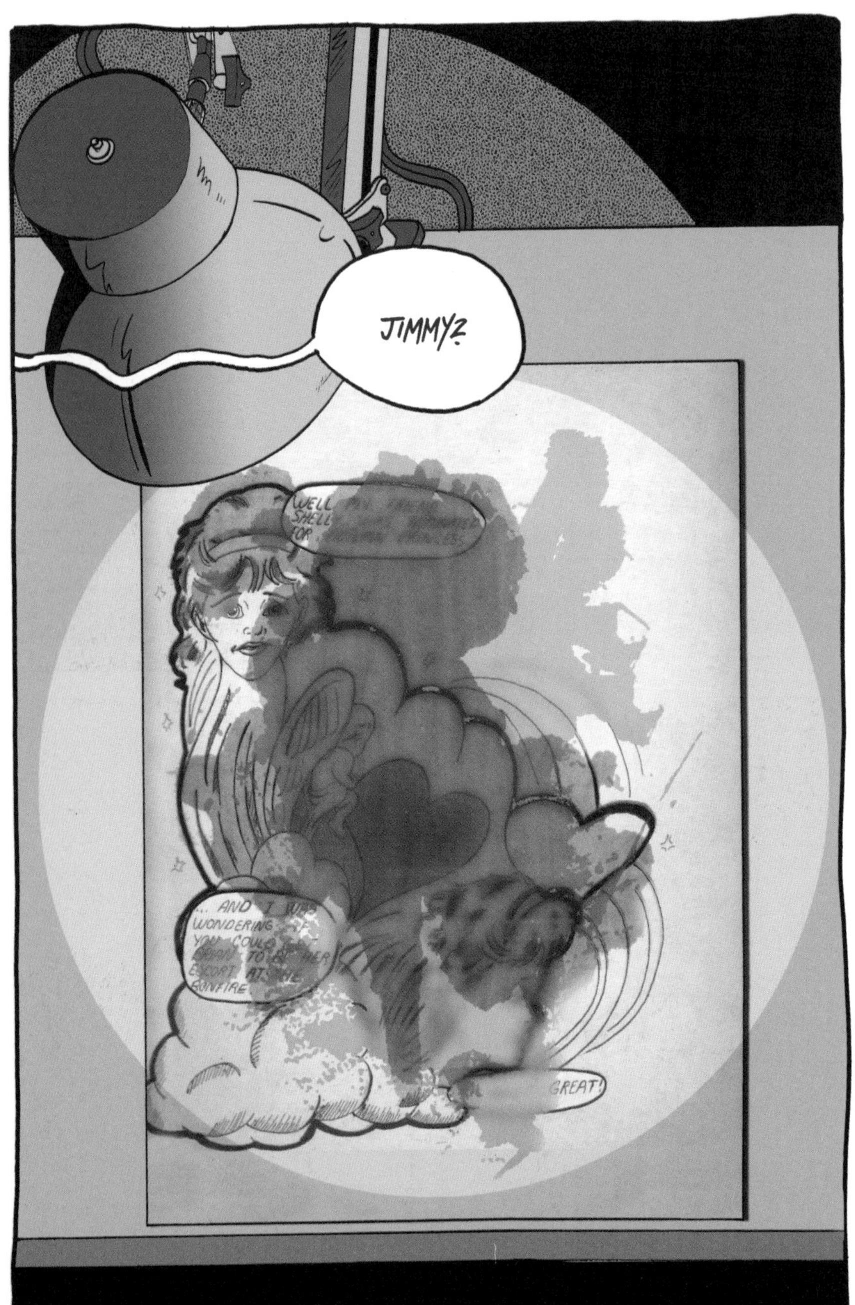
JIMMY?
WELL
SHELL
FOR
... AND I WAS WONDERING IF YOU COULD
TO BE HER ESCORT AT THE BONFIRE
GREAT!

YOU'VE BEEN SITTING THERE FOR HOURS, BUT NOT REALLY DRAWING...
...AND YOU'VE BEEN SO MOPEY.

DO YOU WANT TO TALK ABOUT SOMETHING?

NO. IT'S OKAY... I'M FINE.
I THINK I'LL JUST TAKE A WALK AND CLEAR MY HEAD.

Y'know WHAT? Forget my earlier ADVICE...
...Just give up.
DON'T LISTEN TO HIM! IT WILL GET BETTER!
NO! THERE'S NO POINT! IT ALL FADES AWAY.

Just give up.
EVERYTHING DOES NOT FADE AWAY!
YES, IT DOES! HIS GIRLFRIEND! HIS COMIC! MARNIE! ALL GONE!

Just give up.
STOP THE SELF-PITY. THINK OF THE STARVING CHILDREN!
SHUT UP ABOUT THE STARVING CHILDREN!

Just give up.
JUST BE PERFECT, AND IT'LL BE FINE!
NOTHING WILL EVER BE FINE AGAIN...
JUST.
GIVE.
UP.

ENOUGH!

Whew!

HEY, DAD... I NEED A LIFT.
OKAY, WHERE DO YOU NEED TO GO?

THE COMIC BOOK STORE.
I NEED TO ASK THE OWNER FOR HELP.

HELP?
WHAT KIND OF HELP DO YOU NEED?

I NEED TO START OVER.
OKAAAAY...
GEMA BOOKS

WELL, HOW CAN I HELP?
I NEED TO KNOW ALL OF IT.

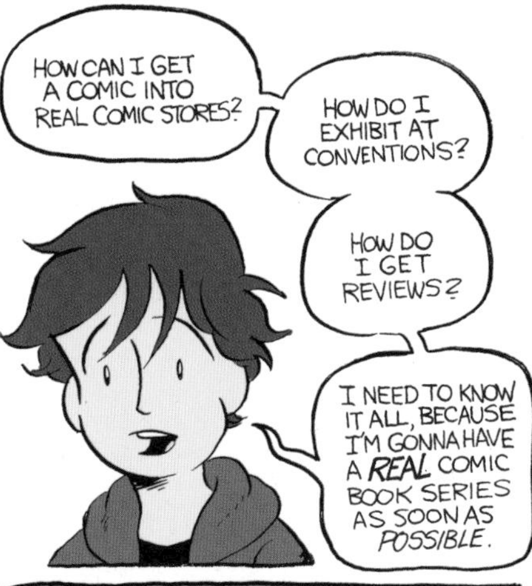
HOW CAN I GET A COMIC INTO REAL COMIC STORES?
HOW DO I EXHIBIT AT CONVENTIONS?
HOW DO I GET REVIEWS?
I NEED TO KNOW IT ALL, BECAUSE I'M GONNA HAVE A *REAL* COMIC BOOK SERIES AS SOON AS *POSSIBLE*.

WELL, I GOTTA GIVE IT TO YOU... YOU SURE ARE PERSISTENT.
ACTUALLY, I'M JUST TOO DUMB TO QUIT.

SO, DO YOU HAVE AN IDEA FOR THIS COMIC BOOK?
I SURE DO.

GREAT! I'VE ALWAYS WONDERED WHERE YOU CREATIVE TYPES GET YOUR IDEAS...
...BUT I GUESS IT'S JUST A MYSTERY.

NOPE.
I KNOW EXACTLY WHERE MY IDEA CAME FROM...

...I GOT IT FROM A FRIEND.

YOU NEED AN IDEA THAT'LL REALLY GRAB PEOPLE, Y'KNOW?
SOMETHING DIFFERENT!
OH! I KNOW...
YOU SHOULD WRITE A COMIC BOOK...
...ABOUT US!
THAT'S the DUMBEST IDEA I'VE EVER HEARD!

I'M NOT GONNA GET RICH WRITING A COMIC BOOK "ABOUT US."
WHAT? YOU'RE NOT TRYING TO GET RICH! THERE'S NO WAY THAT'S WHY YOU'RE DOING THIS.
WELL, NO...
...OF COURSE NOT.
THEN DON'T PRETEND LIKE IT IS.

LOOK, I KNOW YOU BUSTED YOUR BUTT TO MAKE THOSE PAGES.

I DID.
WELL THEN, FOR ALL THAT WORK, YOU SHOULD MAKE THEM MORE YOU, Y'KNOW?
SAY SOMETHING IMPORTANT.

THEY PROBABLY WANT ME TO BE A DOCTOR...
...OR A LAWYER.
... TELL SOMEONE YOU LOVE THEM...
SOMETHING REAL. SOMETHING THAT'S NOT A CARTOONIST.
HOW CAN WE HELP?

OKAY. THAT'S ENOUGH.
... OR TELL SOMEONE OFF...
SISTER I HAVE ANOTHER OBSERVATION.
CHRIS McCONNELL IS A-
RRRIIING

DEAR DIARY MOMENT
~SIGH~ OKAY YOU WEIRDO
NO!
HERE!
...OR JUST TELL SOMEONE... "I KNOW EVERYTHING SUCKS RIGHT NOW..."
YUCK
LIKE THIS?
OKAY. YEAH THAT WAS GROSS.
IT AND...

... BUT TRUST ME...

"...IT'S GONNA BE OKAY."

OKAY. HERE WE GO...

I STILL HAVE MY DESK...
...SOME PENCILS...
...SOME PAPER...

MY HEART'S BROKEN, ALL OF MY PREVIOUS WORK IS PRETTY MUCH USELESS...
...AND I'M YEARS AWAY FROM A GOAL THAT MIGHT NOT EVEN BE ATTAINABLE.

FEELS GOOD HAVING THE HOME COURT ADVANTAGE.

ANYWAY, I CAN'T THINK ABOUT ALL OF THAT...
...ALL I CAN FOCUS ON IS WHAT IS HERE AND NOW...

...AND RIGHT HERE...
...RIGHT NOW...

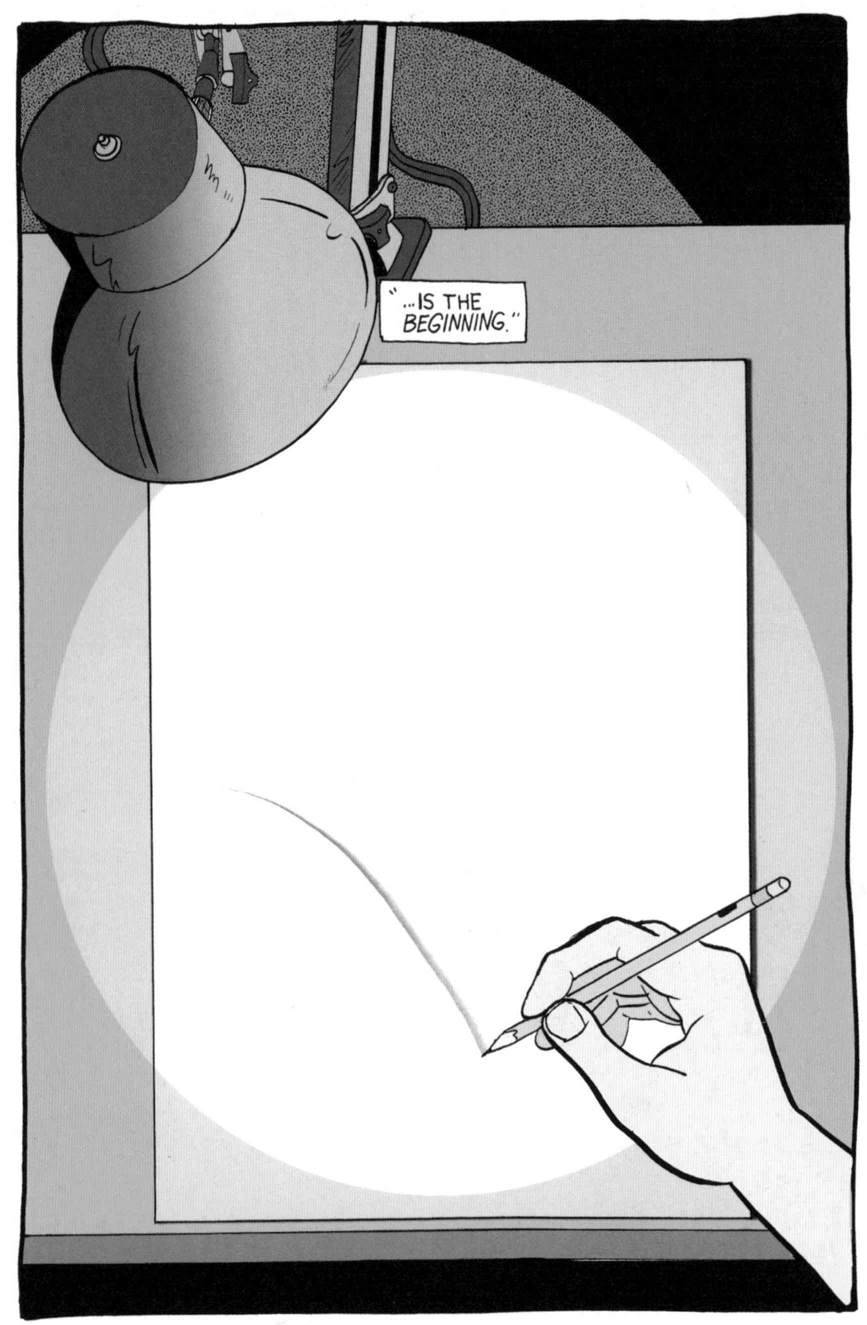
"...IS THE BEGINNING."

AUTHOR'S NOTE

The Dumbest Idea Ever! is my story. And it's a story about beginnings. This book takes place primarily between the years 1985–1990, and it's set in Girardville, a small, economically struggling coal-mining town in northeastern Pennsylvania. My hometown can be pretty rough, but it was also a fun place to grow up.

I'm the only child of a former coal miner and a homemaker. By the time I was three, my mom had taught me to read using homemade flash cards and by reading me Charles Schulz's comic strip, *Peanuts*. I loved *Peanuts*, and I would sometimes take Mom's flash cards and arrange them to make my own comic strip stories. This, along with the fact that my dad grew up reading comic books, cemented my interest in comics.

My first attempt at writing a comic book was a mash-up of *Star Wars* and *Lord of the Rings*. It took about a month to produce three pages, but it was worth it because I was pretty sure they were genius. Before I unleashed my story on the world (or finished it for that matter), I showed it to my friend Tony to get his opinion. He politely informed me that my story was horrible and that no one on earth would ever read it. Then he made the statement that would change my life: "Why don't you write a comic book about us?"

At the time, I thought this was a really dumb idea. But not having any better ones, I did it anyway.

And I'm glad I did — because eventually I discovered the power of Tony's advice. When I did write comic books about us — about real life — I could reach people who might not otherwise read comics.

So I studied, I learned, and by the time I was twenty I was able to self-publish a new version of my *Shades of Gray* comic, which reached a nationwide audience through comic book stores. I put one in an envelope and sent it to Tony, who was then at Johns Hopkins medical center battling leukemia.

Not long after, I got a call from Ellen Toole. Tony had passed away. That comic book turned out to be the last present I was able to give him.

Which still makes me sad. I think about him every day.

But this is a story about beginnings.

Now I'm a professional cartoonist. My Amelia Rules! series has won awards, been translated into other languages, and even became a *New York Times* bestseller. As part of my job, I go around the country speaking at schools and libraries and conventions, and I tell kids the story of how Tony suggested I write about us. I even told it to Ellen's daughter at an assembly at her school. And every time I'm getting ready to leave an event, I see kids with pens and paper, scribbling furiously, trying to capture their own visions, putting their own stories down on paper.

And I watch the story begin again.

ABOUT THE AUTHOR

Jimmy Gownley began writing and drawing comics at age fifteen and has been nominated for the Eisner Award eleven times. In 2001, his hit series Amelia Rules! was released amid a flurry of rave reviews. He cofounded the organization Kids Love Comics, which works to promote comic books and graphic novels as valuable tools for literacy and education in schools, libraries, and at home. Jimmy lives in Harrisburg, Pennsylvania.